Language in Centers
Kids Communicating

by
Laverne Warner and Ken Craycraft

Illustrated by Darcy Tom

Cover by Janet Skiles

Copyright © Good Apple, 1991

ISBN No. 0-86653-616-7

Printing No. 987654321

Good Apple
1204 Buchanan St., Box 299
Carthage, IL 62321-0299

SIMON & SCHUSTER *A Paramount Communications Company*

CHADDADDY

1 Day of Spring

flowers grow in spring.

I Like to Pick Them.
What KinD of Things grow
In Sring?
Trees, grass, flowers,

1)
2)
3)

Dad,
I know you're preety
foxy, But you got to
Be tough,

ii

Dedication

For Rachelle and Warner Matt Phelps and Chad Craycraft who may author their own books someday.

What It All Means

There are many times that we look around,
When it seems that problems are all that can be found.
In our unrelinquishing efforts to make things right,
There is always temptation to give up the fight.

Why should the educator bear the cross,
If the efforts seem to be a loss?
It's time for all to do their part,
Even though some don't know where to start.

But each of us in life has a place,
And more responsibility than taking up space.
It is the courage to follow what we feel,
To reach beyond, to make dreams real.

Children are nature's greatest prize,
You can feel it in their touch and see it in their eyes.
No effort is too small and all are worthwhile,
Because it's impossible to *outgive* the love of a child.

Thank you, Rachelle, Warner, and Chad

Acknowledgements

Thanks are in order to Tracy Rowley and Kay Timme for their contributions to our book. We also thank all of the graduate and undergraduate students at Sam Houston State University for sharing teaching ideas with us and encouraging us to be better than we have to be.

GA1335

Table of Contents

GA1335

Introduction

"Luck! Duck! Tuck! Muck! Buck! Wuck! Juck! Suck!" chants the three-year-old in the grocery cart as her mother wheels her around the store.

"Hickory, dickory, dock, the mouse runs up the spock! Hickory, dickory, dock, the mouse runs up the sock! Hickory, dickory, dock, the mouse runs up the trock!" laughs another child in the sandbox.

How children come to know the language, how they internalize it, and how they use language under a variety of circumstances are areas of intense study for linguists, and both preschool and public school teachers can profit by the knowledge linguists share. By understanding what children can do with language, classroom activities and experiences can be developed which allow children's language to improve and expand.

Children come to preschool classrooms and public schools knowing quite a bit about language. By age four or five, they have internalized most of the rule system of the language. They have a speaking vocabulary of 2000 words or more, and just like adults, they understand even more words than they use. Preschoolers have a basic knowledge of the appropriate social uses of language. They can also conduct simple conversations, and most adults who take the time to listen and converse with youngsters are often surprised to discover what children actually know.

GA1335

An emerging educational trend utilizes this spontaneous language as a learning vehicle to improve the growth of language in classrooms. Allowing children to use their own natural oral language as a foundation and as a transition for moving to literacy experiences focuses on what children can already do, rather than attempting to teach them something that is difficult for them to understand. Helping children to relate new information to knowledge that they already have is a sound teaching principle, one that is supported by numerous research studies. As a consequence, learning becomes more relevant to children and to any learner for that matter.

Comprehending the need for relevant learning is easy if one can remember being required to memorize a fact or formula that had no meaning until the information was actually used in a life experience. Reading a book or travel brochure about another culture is not as meaningful to travelers until they have an opportunity to visit the country or culture and experience it first hand. Information comes to life! For children, this "coming to life" feeling is essential to the quality of learning. Doing a work sheet which focuses on the letter *b* is never as appealing as writing a *b* in a story about a bear which children have composed themselves.

This trend toward relevant language learning is called wholistic language—using natural language in many different ways in many different circumstances. Encourage children to improve their vocabulary through dramatic play, hearing good stories, talking to other children as well as adults, using poems, finger plays, songs and chants, and by introducing children to new information and knowledge with hands-on activities. These are all techniques teachers and caretakers use to enhance children's oral language.

Moving to reading and writing is a natural outgrowth of all of the previously mentioned language experiences, because adults can say "Draw a picture about your favorite part in the story" or "Let's see if we can write down what we just talked about" or "I bet you can write Goldilocks' name by looking at her name on the book cover." When children observe a need for written language, then children will use written language. Placing "special sheets" in the Grocery Store Center, for example, requires children to read or pretend to read the information on them. Preparing menus for an impromptu restaurant dramatic play scene again requires "reading" of the menu, and for the child who is the waiter or waitress, "writing" is expected.

Preschool and primary grade teachers have traditionally placed appropriate labels around their classrooms to help children observe the language/symbol connection.

GA1335

Knowing that the words *door, chair, table, desk, flag, wall, fish, plants, books,* etc., all indicate the names of the items they adorn is but one methodical way that teachers call attention to the printed word. But charting a favorite nursery rhyme, such as "Humpty Dumpty," or printing the words to "This Old Man" on an overhead transparency or onto pictures the children have drawn to accompany the song are also effective devices for calling attention to the sound/word connection.

Many preschool children learn to read in this global fashion by trying to make sense of the print in their environment. The emphasis on relevant reading and writing in children's play and day-to-day activities is a powerful tool which adults can utilize in and out of the classroom. Learning, then, becomes the child's need to know, the child's desire to discover the meaning of environmental print.

This Old Man

This old man
He played one,
He played Knick-Knack
On my thumb,
With a Knick-Knack,
Paddy-whack,
Give a dog a bone.
This old man
Came rolling home.

Eventually, children will need formal instruction in reading and writing. But until the time that formal instruction is actually necessary, allowing them to learn through play experiences which resemble life experiences is developmentally appropriate.

What this book attempts to do is to share information about the use of routine and special classroom centers which will assist children in making the sound/symbol connection. A suitable question to ask is "Why use centers?" The answer is simple: centers provide an equal opportunity for all children in the classroom to interact with one another at one time or another.

Here are some concrete examples to support our answer. Rosey may always choose the Block Center, but eventually every other child will be in the Block Center with Rosey. The oral and nonverbal interactions Rosey has with these children assists her language development and her ability to learn. On the other hand, Cassandra may switch centers on a regular basis.

What Cassandra learns in the Housekeeping Center will be different from what she learns in the Manipulatives Center. The vocabulary she acquires with manipulatives about length, width, size, shape, color, and other attributes will enhance the vocabulary she uses when she chooses the Science Center. When children play together in centers, the interaction is social. Yes, but it is also important because of its cognitive value.

By providing language-rich activities in classroom centers, teachers and caregivers are offering children more opportunities to learn. When children encounter other  children who know more than they know, they learn from others. A comparison can be drawn with adult learning when we listen to documentaries on television or attend public forums and seminars to acquire knowledge from experts. By asking questions, which is another form of interaction, adults learn even more. Of course, children have not acquired all of the subtleties of conversing and question-asking behaviors. Classroom centers, however, give them a place to begin this important acquisition of knowledge.

What *Language in Centers* does is describe the use of centers and center activity to enhance language development for preschool/primary children. The book is divided into two major sections: (1) a description of centers which are traditional ones teachers use on a regular basis, and (2) a description of centers which are developed around thematic topics usually discussed in preschool and primary classrooms. In each center discussion unit, the stated purposes for the centers are included, plus a suggested floor plan, materials, and books.

A description of activities at two levels are presented. One level is appropriate for preschool and kindergarten classrooms; they are usually activities which use oral language. The second, more difficult level is appropriate for first and second grade classrooms and requires more direct instruction. Adults who are using this book will need to make judicious decisions on a regular basis about the activities and how appropriate they are for each group of children they are working with.

Our hope is that you will consider some of our ideas for enhancing language in your classroom. The benefit, of course, is what children will learn as a by-product of your efforts.

GA1335

The Role of Adults in the Classroom

Encouraging natural language in preschool/primary classrooms means that adults must plan for it to happen. Five specific ways that teachers develop wholistic language processes are (1) preparing the environment for interaction to occur; (2) planning literacy experiences which are an outgrowth of routine and play activities; (3) recognizing the role of self-expression as a foundation for language literacy; (4) understanding when children need challenges; and (5) communicating to parents about children's growth. A discussion of these five strategies follows.

Preparing the Environment for Interaction to Occur. Using classroom centers is an ideal organizational plan to allow for children's interactions. Centers which are typically found in classrooms for young children are the Housekeeping Center, Manipulatives Center, Art Center, Book Corner, Puppet Center, Grocery Store Center, and the Math and Science Centers. Other centers are usually thematic in nature and change throughout the year, based on children's interests and topics of curriculum study. Many could be included, but *Language in Centers* focuses on the Nursery Rhymes Center, Family Relationships Center, School Center, Neighborhood Center, Transportation Center, Health and Safety Center, Communication and Sounds Center, Protecting the Environment Center, Farm and Ranch Center, and Insect Center. When children are in centers, they are interacting. When they are interacting with others, they are learning.

ix

GA1335

Planning Literacy Experiences. Typical interactions between children are verbal ones. Language experts agree that oral language should serve as a foundation for learning and, for children, all learning begins orally. But eventually, the language user must learn about reading and writing, and the adults who work with children need to use a variety of resources to interest children in print.

Adding activities to routines and center play which require children to explore print is one effective technique which focuses on the need for print without being threatening to children. Specific strategies for promoting print are developing a daily written schedule with children; using a centers selection board which children must "read" in order to choose the center they move to; writing messages to children; and providing lifelike experiences which require knowledge of print to include in each of the centers. Having a sink/float chart on the math and science table, for example, allows children to classify objects into two categories and at the same time, they see the words *sink* and *float* while they are experimenting. Preschool and primary teachers have traditionally placed printed labels around their classrooms in order to call attention to the printed word in relationship to the child's environment.

Recognizing the Role of Self-Expression. Preschool children will not begin reading and writing immediately. The process is a gradual one which begins in children's needs to express themselves. Just as children babble and coo before they talk, so do they scribble and draw before they read and write. Adults will understand that scribbling and artwork are precursors of reading and writing. Teachers should capitalize on these first attempts at self-expression and call them writing or reading. Suggesting to children that their marks on paper have meaning calls attention to the process of writing.

Another way to establish the print/sound connection is to ask the children to "read" their scribbles. Encourage children to write notes to you or to another child in the classroom. Or begin writing children notes which have a combination of words and pictures on them which can be read. A reminder to David that it's his day to feed the fish could simply be a picture of a fish in a fishbowl with the accompanying words *Feed the fish*. Label children pictures with captions or sentences about their art. If you have time or if you have an aid in the classroom, allow children to dictate stories about their art which can be taken home to their parents. Just by asking children to write their names on their pictures could be the turning point in helping them recognize that print has a message.

GA1335

Understanding the Challenges Children Need. Generally children will exhibit behaviors which indicate that they are ready to learn more. Some children will be very plain about their request, "Teach me to read." Some children will be reading without really knowing that they are doing so. Others will enjoy stories over and over again without ever being ready to move into reading or writing. At whatever level children are, teachers should be prepared to provide activities which will assist children in understanding print symbols.

One child may need to be told "You are reading." Another child may need to find her name from among all of the name tags of her classmates. Another child could be encouraged to find a favorite book from among a stack of books and told in the process that he "read" the book's title. True, he may have recognized the book because of other features—its color or the pictures on the cover—but he found the book nevertheless, and calling this behavior "reading" helps children understand what reading is all about. Many teachers put their hand under the line of print they are reading to children so that a connection can be made more easily.

Occasionally, group experiences are as successful as any technique teachers use. Asking small groups of children to write a letter to the principal about classroom events or to record sentences about their trip to the fire station points out the need for print. The specific communication known as literacy will need to be demonstrated time and again for children to help them understand the process.

Communicating to Parents. One of the teacher's most important roles is communicating to parents. Parents often have high expectations that their children will be learning to read and write at an early age, and they do not always understand the developmental process which occurs for children to achieve literacy. Teachers can alleviate some of the concerns which parents have about their children. Most public school classrooms prepare report cards for parents, but child care centers do not always follow this practice. Notes, parent-teacher conferences, telephone calls, informal chats, newsletters, checklists, or some other reporting system will be necessary when teaching in preschool/primary classrooms.

Sometimes it becomes important to inform parents about literacy and the developmental process that children go through to acquire knowledge of print. When parents of preschool children comprehend the teaching strategies used with the wholistic language approach, they can begin to understand how they can also use a variety of home routines and activities to encourage the child's interest in print. They also become aware of information children already know about print and capitalize on reinforcing that knowledge from time to time. The teacher should make decisions about appropriate activities from *Language in Centers* to share with parents so that classroom language experiences can be extended into the home routine.

GA1335

Using Manuscript

Children's first writing attempts should be with print that they invent. From a developmental perspective, this writing will only vaguely resemble adult print. In time children do begin to write strings of letters which are recognizable, but the message is lost because all of the letters may be the same or a combination of two or three letters. Eventually, children will need manuscript models to follow and specific instruction in manuscript writing, though formal instruction is not actually needed until first grade. What should the adult do until that time arrives? Here are some guidelines to consider.

1. Provide charts which show manuscript handwriting in the classroom. Commercial varieties are available, but preparing a teacher-made chart resembling the manuscript forms shown on the next page is as effective.

2. Model good manuscript forms for the children. Following this guideline probably means that the teacher will need to do some practice prior to working with children in classroom settings.

3. Except where capital letters are necessary, use lowercase forms. The rationale for this suggestion is that print in preprimers and first readers is in lowercase form, and children will be able to make the transition to beginning reading more quickly if there are similarities in the writing forms they use and those they observe in texts.

4. Encourage children to use their own judgement about how words sound and how they are to be spelled (often referred to as "invented spelling"). If children become unduly concerned about how words are to be spelled at an early age, they may lose sight of the intent of writing, its message.

5. Do not expect children to begin writing on lined paper. Unlined paper is a more suitable choice, because children can write letters without having to be concerned about keeping print within lines, a variable which adds difficulty to the writing of letters.

GA1335

I wish you a happy
summer. To Miss Warner
From Mike
I thank you are
my best Teacher I'v
ever had. I hate to
go to the second grade
But I hope I pass.

Love
Mike

2

Aa Bb Cc Dd
Ee Ff Gg Hh
Ii Jj Kk Ll
Mm Nn Oo Pp
Qq Rr Ss Tt
Uu Vv Ww
Xx Yy Zz ?
1 2 3 4 5 6 7 8 9 10

Part I
Routine Year-Round Centers

Introduction

Planning stationary centers of interest in the classroom is desirable because of the need to provide consistency and routine to classroom activity. Teachers generally decide before the school year begins where they want furniture placed and what kinds of learning will occur in their classrooms. By establishing several centers which will remain stable throughout the year, the teacher can define learning activities, quiet and noisy areas of the classroom, traffic flow, how many children can be together at a time, and which rules will guide their use.

The classroom environment's plan serves as an organizing structure which assists the teacher in classroom management as well as an attractive agent to entice children to learn. Teachers do not have to continually change their classroom in order to facilitate learning. Classroom learning can occur by adding more challenging materials to centers or by interacting with children in centers. One or two centers will change because of the topical nature of study in classrooms of young children, but these change once or twice monthly. Otherwise, teachers should not spend all of their time planning and changing the environment in the classroom. Needless to say, this practice is foolhardy.

Tips for Setting Up Centers:

1. Consider the traffic flow in the classroom. Group quiet centers with other quiet centers.

2. Remember to leave room for a large circle area so that all children can sit together in a group if necessary.

3. Mark the center clearly with its name accompanied with a picture for non-readers (here's another relevant way to use print).

4. Have a Center Selection Board where children can place their names on the board to indicate where they will be playing.

5. Because it is necessary to limit the number of children in any given center, a number could be placed by the name of the center on the Center Board so that children will know when the limit has been reached.

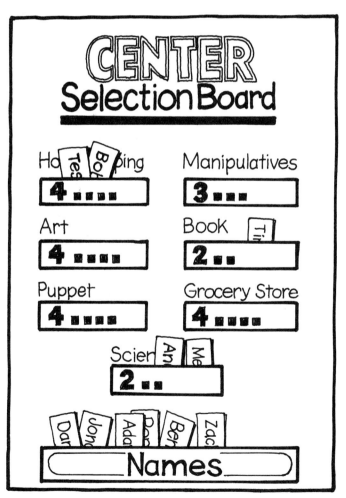

Housekeeping Center

The Housekeeping Center is a traditional center in the prekindergarten and kindergarten grades, but its use can be beneficial to the primary grades as well. Essentially it serves as a bridge from the home to school. Children are able to role-play what they know best, their home lives. They take on the roles which they observe most closely, and they find an easy avenue to expression through familiar activities and routines. Playing and learning in the Housekeeping Center is safe and nonthreatening.

The purposes of the Housekeeping Center are as follows:

To give children an opportunity to imitate family roles with which they are most familiar

To allow children to interact with one another just as families would

To assist children in understanding that family structures and family activities are unique to individual families

To provide experiences which will serve as a foundation for play interactions with other center areas in the classroom, such as the Grocery Store Center, the Family Relationships Center or the Neighborhood Center

Here's what you need to prepare the Housekeeping Center.

Child-sized kitchen and bedroom furniture (commercial varieties are available, but these can be prepared by enterprising parents or senior citizens)

Plastic dishes, pots and pans, and other kitchen equipment and utensils (child-sized varieties are best, but discarded items from the teacher's own kitchen could be substituted if these were all that were available)

Dolls (representing several races), cribs, carriages, plastic baby bottles, blankets, pillows and other equipment which will enhance doll play

Walls for the "house" (these might possibly be room dividers or bulletin boards, but large cardboard boxes might serve the purpose equally well)

Pictures, plastic flowers, plastic food items (or ones made from papier-mâché), magazine racks, wastebaskets, wind chimes, curtains, bedspreads, rugs, table doilies, and other ornamental items to decorate the "home"

Empty plastic and cardboard containers of commercial products (detergents, cereals, crackers, toothpaste containers, etc., much like the items one would find in the Grocery Store Center)

Prop boxes (large boxes which include materials to accompany specific play themes such as a birthday party, Thanksgiving dinner, Christmas, etc.)

GA1335

A typical floor plan for the Housekeeping Center might look like the following:

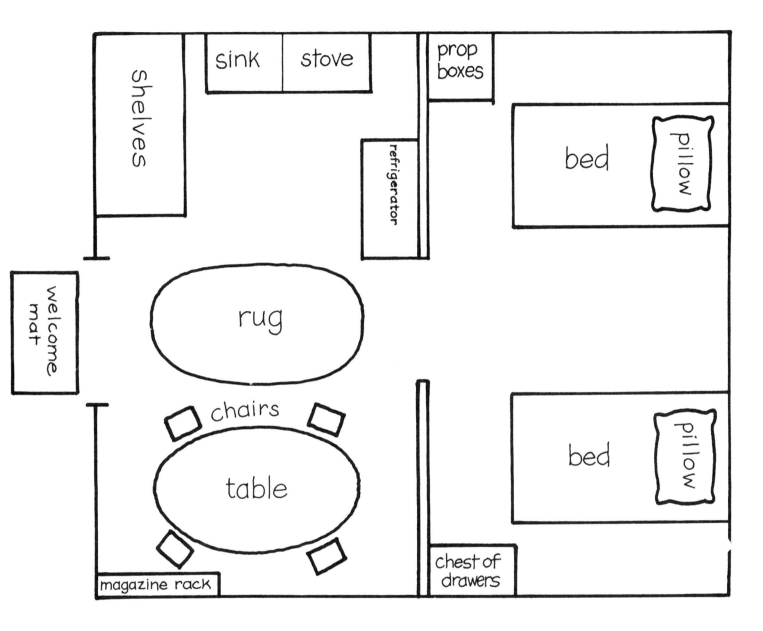

Try some of these activities to enhance language learning.

Magazine Magic—The book rack should be filled with many magazines where children can feel free to cut and paste. Encourage the children who wish to use the center to pretend they are in a room in their home and to decorate it to appear like it actually looks or the way they would like it to look by cutting out pictures from the magazines and gluing them onto a large piece of manila paper. Once the room is complete, the children can share their ideas and pictures with others. Also, the teacher may want to display similar rooms together (bedrooms, kitchens, dens, etc.) and ask children to discuss common features.

Children who are studying letter recognition can cut out pictures of items found in the house that begin with a certain sound or letter individually or with a group of children. Display the collages as part of the decor of the Housekeeping Center.

Newspaper Corner—All kinds of newspapers should be displayed for children to use. To encourage verbal and prediction skills, the children can select an action picture of an animal or person and tell other children in this section what they think is happening.

An activity to promote sequencing skills would be for the teacher to cut out cartoon strips, laminate them and have the children place them in the order they think they belong. As a self-checking device, each cartoon strip can be numbered in the correct order. An extension of this activity could be to have the children create their own cartoon strips and verbally describe the events to other children or even act out the ideas.

Promote listening skills by selecting a few newspapers and record sounds that could be associated with the pictures on a cassette recorder. The children could play the sound, locate the picture and listen to a follow-up response to check for accuracy by color-coding the correct one and identifying the color on the tape.

Select a series of pictures from the newspapers representing a variety of expressions. The children can select a picture and tell what they think is happening or act out what they think is happening.

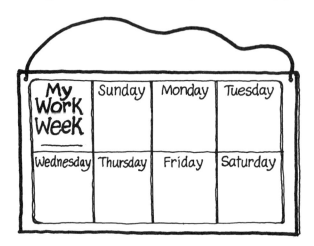

A Week of Work—The teacher should take a piece of tagboard and divide it into seven sections. In each section, the day of the week should be written. Then the children should take pictures from magazines or draw the work they are responsible for at home on that particular day of the week. To enable the children to display their finished product at home, a piece of yarn could be attached to each end of their chart.

And the List Goes On—One activity for most households is making a grocery list. Usually, most parents or guardians plan what they purchase based on what is on sale and what they need. Working in small groups, the children can cut pictures from grocery ads, glue them on a piece of paper and make their own grocery lists. Encourage them to discuss what is needed and to choose the types of products a family would need. Ask them to guess why large numbers of certain items are not bought (for example, fruit, milk, bread, etc.) Older children may choose to actually write their own lists or label the pictures they choose.

Creating a Household Product Book—To encourage children to be more aware of the many products they use at home, develop a home product book. The small groups of children should take several pieces of paper and then cut and paste pictures that represent the products used in the bathroom, bedroom, the kitchen, the den, etc. Each room should be represented by a separate page. If the teacher chooses to have each child develop individual books, encourage small groups of children to compare the items they selected and to tell why the particular product is used in a particular room at their household.

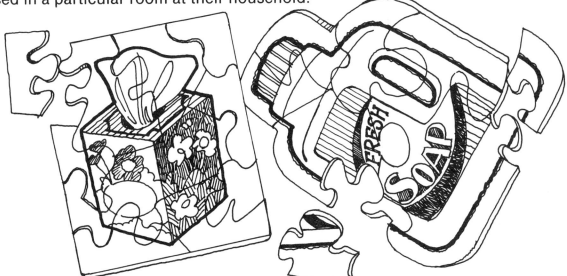

Puzzle Me Not—Create household product puzzles by using cardboard cartons from empty product containers or drawing pictures of household products and gluing them on sections of a poster board, laminating them and then cutting each in several puzzle pieces. When two or more children are working in this area, a child can complete the puzzle and tell another about the product (for example, where it is found in the house, how it is used and whether or not it is safe). Should the caregiver desire, the puzzles can be thematic by relating to a certain room, a specific type of product or those requiring specific types of actions when used.

"Ring, Ring"—Help children develop proper phone manners and communication skills for informal and emergency situations. To complete the following activities, two phones will be necessary. (Note: Many phone companies loan phone equipment to public school classrooms which operate realistically with dial tones, rings, and busy signals.

Since the phones will be available for children to play with at any time, activity during the first few days should simply allow children to play with the phones in any way they choose. By observing children through these informal activities, the teacher can determine what the children actually know about telephones and their uses.

Once this introductory period is over, a simple screen should be placed between the two phones. Located beside one phone will be a group of pictures. The pictures can be of people, places or things. One child is to select a laminated picture and then begin to describe what it is (using the phone) without actually naming it. Colors, shapes, actions or other general clues should be encouraged. When the child receiving the clues is successful in identifying the picture, the children are to trade places and repeat these steps.

An activity to promote the skill of sequencing is to teach children important phone numbers and the proper ways they are to be used. Since it is critical to stress the proper use of emergency phone numbers, the adult should incorporate formal instruction as well as many opportunities to practice in the Housekeeping Center. Several cards depicting emergency versus nonemergency situations could be presented and the children asked what they should do. In cases where emergency situations are depicted, the children should demonstrate understanding by actually dialing 911 on the phone and reporting the appropriate information.

Photo Phone Books can be made so that children can record their phone numbers and those of the fire fighter, doctor, and the 911 emergency number, etc. The phone books could be cut in a telephone shape. Young children will need to have these precut, but older children could trace and cut out their own patterns.

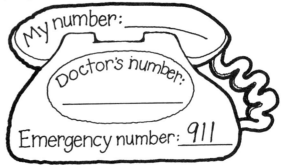

My number: _____
Doctor's number: _____
Emergency number: 911

Encourage children to learn their home phone numbers and practice dialing from the center. In the cases where a phone does not exist in the home, the children can learn the number of a neighbor or relative. Again, proper phone manners should be stressed for the children to practice. The teacher may want to create a set of cards with certain messages to leave for another person (telling a neighbor you have received his or her mail and when it is convenient to pick it up, inviting someone over to play during certain hours, etc.).

GA1335

We Get Letters!—Encourage youngsters to write letters to other children in the classroom while they are playing in the Housekeeping Center. Attach a mailbox to the Housekeeping Center so that a pretend mail carrier can pick it up to take to the child. If children are very young, "writing" can be pictures which are drawn onto a piece of paper. First and second graders can make attempts to write letters or stories for their classmates. Add stationery and note pads to the center to promote letter writing. Occasionally providing party invitations to the paper stock in the center will make center activity more interesting.

Dear Ben,
Thank you for being my friend and helping me make the nice painting for my sick dog.
Your buddy,
Juan

Keeping a Diary—Purchase a diary to place in the Housekeeping Center. Ask children who are already writing to record on a daily basis what was done in the center while they were playing.

Keep the Home Fires Burning—Encourage children to write stories about their home lives. Recommending a variety of topics to children is useful in challenging them to continue their writing. Here are some suggestions.

The Reason I Like My Mom
My Favorite Pet
Doing Things with Dad
How I Help at Home
My Favorite Room in Our House
What Our Family Does for Fun
My Favorite Toys
How I Play at Home
Who My Neighbors Are

Household Odds and Ends—Other print mediums to include in the Housekeeping Center are recipe books; telephone note pads; message boards (like ones families keep in their kitchens); calendars for setting dental, medical, or other appointments; classroom telephone lists (forming a Classroom Telephone Directory is a challenging activity in itself); lists of chores to be done or instructions for completing household chores.

GA1335

Manipulatives Center

Puzzles, beads, pegs and pegboards, attribute blocks, and other manipulative materials hold an attraction for children that is undeniable. Infants and toddlers are given pounding boards; shape books; boxes for blocks and shape pieces to be dropped into; balls; and other materials, usually brightly colored, so that they can begin using their senses to acquire knowledge. A spillover effect occurs in the preschool and primary years because of the concrete, hands-on nature of the manipulative materials. Using them is just plain fun, and children know it whether they understand their educational value or not. Like flour and sugar in the homemaker's kitchen, the Manipulatives Center is always a staple area in the early childhood classroom.

The purposes of the Manipulatives Center are as follows:

To help children learn important mathematics knowledge about part-whole relationships, counting, patterning, classification, telling time and using money

To provide sensory experiences through materials which have a variety of textures, weights, colors, sizes, shapes, lengths, and widths

To allow children to develop fine muscle control as they experiment with and manipulate materials

To use manipulative materials for problem solving activities (in addition and subtraction, for example) and other mathematical concepts

Here's what you need to prepare a Manipulatives Center:

Puzzles, pegboards, pegs, Lincoln Logs, Tinkertoys, dominoes, checkers, tokens, attribute blocks, beads and strings, scales, rulers, yardsticks, beanbags and other materials which will allow children to construct, count, measure, match, or put together

Many raw materials for counting (beads, buttons, pipe cleaners, straws, etc.)

Teacher-made folder games which children can use for matching, classifying, categorizing, measuring, and counting

Materials that children can use for preparing charts (paper and markers)

Shelves and storage bins (laundry baskets and empty gallon ice-cream containers are especially nice)

Digital and/or wall clock, timers, and cardboard clock faces; play money

GA1335

A typical floor plan for the Manipulatives Center might look like the following:

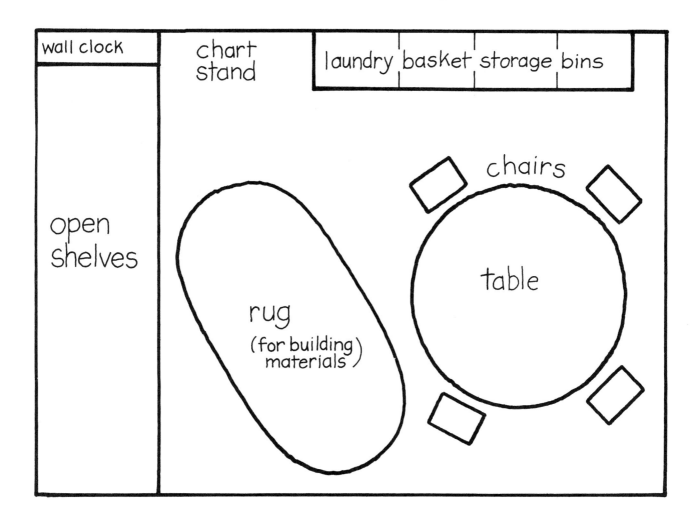

Here are some ideas to try to enhance language learning.

Follow the Leader—In the open area of the learning center, the teacher should place several task cards which depict a series of simple physical activities for the child to attempt. One card could instruct (through picture or words) the child to hop on one foot, tie the shoe of another child, clap to a certain rhythm, march to a particular song, pick up small objects with a spoon requiring the left and then right hand, performing simple physical exercises or any other activity appropriate for the children. Clear the area of any obstacles before doing this activity.

Shape Me But Don't Break Me—On this table, there should be different lengths of yarn for the children to use (or a spool of yarn with safety scissors for children to cut their own lengths) as well as glue and paper for the creation of particular shapes. The caregiver should have a poster board that contains colorful geometric shapes children are expected to know with the names included. Even if the children cannot read, the association of shapes with words will be useful. Then encourage each youngster to re-create the figures on the poster by taking the yarn, making the shape on the construction paper and then gluing it on (coloring is optional). Or you may wish to have the child make the shape with the glue on the paper and then place the yarn on top of the glue. An optional activitiy would be for two children to work together in the creation of the shapes to promote verbal skills relating to a specific task. An extension of this activity would be to place Play-Doh in the Art Center for the children to create shapes with or make up and name shapes of their own.

For children who have been introduced to the alphabet, letters could be formed as well.

Tracing and Cutting—On this table the teacher should provide patterns of shapes and letters for children to trace on different colored construction paper and then cut out. Since the letters will require a higher degree of fine motor skill execution, the teacher should begin with shapes and then add letters. Later she can glue the names of the children on a poster for them to trace and cut out. As an added feature, encourage the children to create a picture with the shapes by gluing them on a piece of contruction paper and then share the picture with a friend in a story form. In addition to verbal skills, the children are working on sequencing and creative expression.

Puzzle Corner—In this area of the learning center, the caregiver should have puzzles reinforcing the different shapes. The colorful shapes should be placed or drawn on a poster board, laminated and then cut into puzzle pieces. Once the children have completed their puzzles, they should tell a friend the names of the shapes.

Those puzzles being created with letters should also include a picture of something that begins with that particular letter. This way, letters and objects are being associated. Each child should be encouraged to identify verbally the pictures on each puzzle which reinforces the sounds the letters make. Keep in mind that the puzzle pieces should be large and not too complex.

GA1335

How Much Can I Hold?—On this particular table, the teacher should have objects of all types and sizes. These can range from coffee cans to vegetable cans to plastic containers to actual measuring devices. The major concepts to promote are comparing (big, bigger, biggest), contrasting (likenesses and differences), and estimating (how many cans of water will this one hold)—all within the developmental limits of the children. Whether you are using water or sand, the children should be allowed to simply explore and experiment freely with the containers. Since two or three children will likely be working together, they already will be discussing how much water or sand each container will hold. After they are allowed to experiment freely, provide the children with paper and encourage them to draw the number of little cans it takes to fill one large can, etc. Also, encourage the children to guess how many little cans it will take to fill another container and so on. If the children can write, they can use numerals instead of actual drawings.

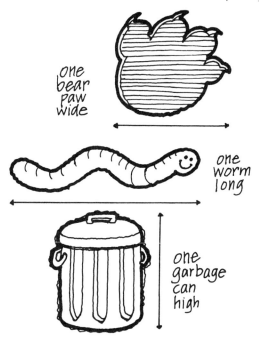

one bear paw wide

one worm long

one garbage can high

How Long Am I?—On this table, or section of a table, the children will be provided with several nonconventional measuring devices. For instance, the teacher may wish to trace or draw a bear's paw to use as a tool, an "inch" worm, Oscar the Grouch's trash can, or any other items she feels the children will like. Then the teacher furnishes each pair of students with a sheet of paper with several items for them to measure. For instance, the teacher will ask the children how many bear paw lengths it is across the table, how many trash cans tall you and your partner are, etc. The children will then share this information with other children and are establishing the basis for measurement.

Books for the Manipulatives Center:

Gillham, Bill, and Susan Hulme. *Let's Look for Shapes.* New York: Coward-McCann, Inc., 1984.

Hoban, Tana. *Circles, Triangles and Squares.* New York: Macmillan Publishing Company, Inc., 1974.

_____ . *Is It Larger? Is It Smaller?* New York: Greenwillow Books, 1985.

_____ . *Shapes, Shapes, Shapes.* New York: Greenwillow Books, 1986.

Art Center

Big, bold splashes of color! Brush strokes which are larger than life! What joy to express oneself with paint and paper! The Art Center is emotionally satisfying! Children can make a statement: "This is who I am!" They dabble with finger paint, paint at the easel with abandon, squeeze Play-Doh with delight, pound emphatically on clay, creating with the skill of any artist. The Art Center means self-expression. Its language is the symbols and scribbles children spread on paper and the representations they design from clay, Play-Doh, or other raw materials. Of all the centers in the classroom, here is the spot for writing to begin, because children can express what they know at the level of expertise they have, however limited. Today children paint; tomorrow, they write.

The purposes of the Art Center are as follows:

To provide opportunities for children to express themselves

To develop fine muscle skills through the use of brushes, markers, crayons, pencils, chalk, and other art media

To allow children in understanding that symbols have meaning

To allow emotional outlets for tensions and daily stressors children experience at school and in their homes

To underscore the aesthetic value of individual creations

Here's what you need to prepare an Art Center.

Easels (at least two, but the more classrooms can afford, the better)

Child-sized tables and chairs

Bulletin board or wall space for displaying children's artwork

Open shelves for storage of art materials

Brushes, paints, crayons, markers, pencils, paper of all types (large selections are best), glue or glue sticks, children's scissors, finger paints and numerous assortments of commercial art materials

An abundance of raw materials (discarded bits of yarn, string, fabric, cotton balls, Styrofoam cups, glitter, Popsicle sticks, pipe cleaners, egg cartons, aluminum foil, cellophane, buttons, boxes, Styrofoam packing "worms," cardboard, scraps of paper, wrapping paper), cookie cutters, sets of printing materials, homemade playdough, and the list of items is endless

Eight to ten child-sized paint smocks and old towels or rags for cleanup chores

Cord and clothespins for hanging pictures to dry

Tile flooring (or plastic covering for floor areas which will be harmed by spilled paint)

A typical floor plan for the Art Center might look like the following:

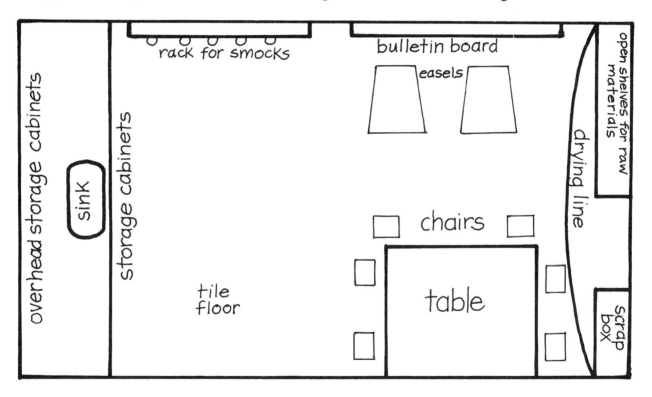

Here are some ideas to try to enhance language learning.

Odd Paintings—Encourage children to look for unusual objects on their way to school, on the playground area, or at home and to bring them to class (pinecones, leaves, acorns, seashells, etc.). Then the children can dip the objects in paint and press them on pieces of paper. The results will be unusual shapes and patterns. The children will be learning more about the different ways individuals can express themselves through art. Telling or dictating creative stories about the picture designs will extend the language learning.

GA1335

Tracing Letters in Our Names—Prepare name cards for every child in the class on either construction paper or poster board flash cards. Children are to dip their fingers in paint and trace the letters of the alphabet. An alternative to this would be to have the children trace the letters with glue and sprinkle sand on the them. After allowing ample opportunity for drying, the children can dip their fingers in paint and trace over the sanded letters. One or both of the exercises will assist children in learning the shapes of letters. Should a glue stick be used instead of paint, the children can feel what it is like to actually form the letters with a writing utensil. Older children can select their own words to write on the cards.

Colors Everywhere—Have white construction paper available for the children and small containers of paint in the primary colors. The children should then be encouraged to draw pictures of objects that represent the colors (red apple, yellow sun, blue water or sky, etc.). Once the drawings are complete, the child should tell another student about the picture using the names of the colors and objects created. On a separate sheet of white construction paper, allow children to experiment by mixing the primary colors to form a new one. Some will be recognizable and others will not. The purpose is for children to discover how other shades and colors are created.

Trace-a-Picture Art—Provide children with large pieces of manila paper and ask them to trace their hands and/or feet. From these tracings, encourage them to create a picture with their tracings as the focal point and then paint them accordingly. Some of the more apparent objects to suggest or use as a motivational tool for the children could be a hand turkey, a butterfly using the tracings of both hands, or a boat from the tracing of the foot, but children can be creative in their efforts. Once the pictures dry, ask children to make up an oral or written story about their art.

18

Paint a Story—Using easels, allow two or three students to work together to create and illustrate a story. Their creation can be based on a favorite book or just be made up. The children are to discuss what they would like to paint, decide on who should paint what and each be responsible for one segment of the illustration. Or several illustrations for one story might be necessary. After using tempera paints and poster board to complete their assignments, the finished stories can be shared with the caregiver or other class members.

Books for the Art Center:

Emberley, Ed. *Drawing Book of Animals.* Boston: Little, Brown and Co., 1970.

Lopshire, Robert. *The Beginner Book of Things to Make: Fun Stuff You Can Make All by Yourself.* New York: Random House, 1964.

Maestro, Betsy. *The Story of the Statue of Liberty.* New York: Lothrop, Lee & Shepard Books, 1986.

GA1335

Book Corner

The Book Corner is a perennial favorite! Here children can visit the storybook characters they like best—the Three Pigs, Goldilocks, the Gingerbread Man, Chicken Licken, the Little Red Hen, Little Red Riding Hood, and many more. Who knows what wonderment hides in the Book Corner. Only those know who have time to pore over the pictures, scrutinize every page, and interact with lifelong fictional friends.

Children's very existence depends on the doors which literature can open. By laughing, crying, becoming frightened, finding relief, being mystified, sitting precariously between fantasy and reality, and vicariously living the lives their favorite personalities live can children discover the power in the written word. Print becomes story and story becomes embedded deep within children, molding permanently how they will mature. Remembering these literary friends later in life will always bring a poignant memory of childhood.

The purposes of the Book Corner are as follows:

To introduce children to the literary heritage of our culture

To demonstrate the pleasure in looking at pictures and hearing stories read

To allow children to experience the rhythm, repetition, and alliteration of the language

To help children learn how to care for books

To provide models of behavior as described by narratives in a variety of books

To develop the concept that print has meaning

To assist children in learning the beginning-middle-end grammar of stories

Here's what you need to prepare a Book Corner.

Books, books, and more books which are developmentally appropriate for the children being taught

Shelves or display stands for the books

GA1335

Children's magazines and newspapers

Large pillows, beanbag chairs, or comfortable chairs

Optional equipment could include a large bathtub filled with pillows, a hammock (placed close to the floor), a loft area, a tent or a large refrigerator box filled with pillows and a reading lamp inside

A bulletin board with pictures of favorite storybook characters or book jackets or a mobile to mark the Book Corner

A chart showing the proper care of books

A large rug in the area (so that group storytelling can be developed)

An adult-sized rocking chair (for one-on-one storytelling)

A trunk filled with costumes representing some of the children's favorite literary personalities

A typical floor plan for the Book Corner might look like the following:

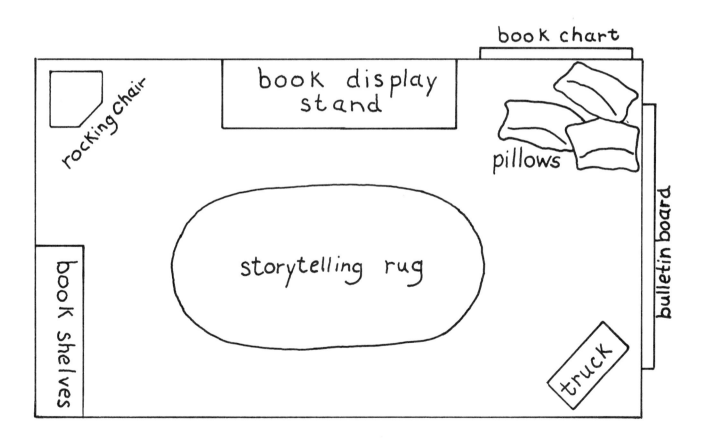

Sloppy Sam and Sara—To introduce the children to the wonderful world of print and the importance of caring for reading materials, a flannel board story should be used to accompany the following poem. After reading and moving the flannel characters the first time, the teacher can allow the children to manipulate the felt figures while reading the story again. Afterwards, she can leave the felt board and characters in a section of the learning center for children to play with on their own.

Sloppy Sam and Sara

Sloppy Sam and Sara
Were people like you and me,
But one thing that made them different;
They were as sloppy as could be.

It made no difference where they went
Or what they were trying to do.
Dirt just seemed to stick to them
From their heads to the bottom of their shoe.

Now when their teacher saw them coming,
She knew she was in a fix.
Because this teacher had lots of books,
And dirt and books don't mix.

But this teacher was very clever;
She would set them straight.
There would be rules for caring for books,
Rules children would not break.

Children love to read you know,
From the beginning to the very end.
Then they want to tell the story,
And the book becomes their friend.

So when the teacher told them
How long a book could last,
If a few simple rules were followed,
And the children caught on fast.

Never bend the pages
Or color or paste or tear.
Always keep them off the floor
And treat them with loving care.

One last thing to remember
Before we read our books,
Our hands should be very clean
To avoid the dirty looks.

Now Sam and Sara were listening
Because they both sure loved to read.
But they knew the teacher was serious;
Her message they would heed.

So now when Sam and Sara read
Their hands are spic and span.
They treat the books like a special friend,
And that was the teacher's plan.

Teacher

23

GA1335

Animal House—Set up an area of the Book Corner which contains materials about animals. Children love to learn about animals and see pictures of them. Two excellent magazines dealing with animals are *Ranger Rick* and *Our Big Back Yard* (for the younger child). Both of these are published by the National Wildlife Federation in Washington, D.C. (1412 Sixteenth Street NW, Washington, D.C. 20036). Not only do these magazines contain large colorful pictures but have activities for children to do.

The teacher may want the animal table to be thematic in nature. For instance, the magazines could lead to a theme of caring for pets or what animals do during the winter, or animals of a particular region of the country. Changing books in the Book Corner is a must if teachers want the area to be attractive and challenging to children. Should the children be nonreaders, the teacher may want to record several stories on cassette tapes for them to play at their leisure. If the children are readers, they can read the books to themselves or take turns reading to each other.

An extension activity would be to have a veterinarian talk to the children about proper pet care and the responsibilities of pet ownership. Should the theme of the center be about animals of the region, a forest ranger could be invited to the class. Not only are children utilizing their listening skills, they are learning more about a particular subject from another source of information.

Later, children can illustrate pictures of their favorite animals, record their own stories on a cassette tape to accompany their illustrations or save their illustrations to collect into a child-made book about animals.

GA1335

Learn with *Weekly Reader*—Provide additional opportunities for independent learning by ordering *Weekly Readers* for children (Field Publications, 245 Long Hill Road, Middletown, Connecticut 06457). Introduce the materials in a large group setting and allow the children to complete the activities in this center. Supplement the theme of each issue by adding other materials to the corner ranging from newspapers to children's books.

A Trunk of Surprises—Provide children with opportunities to assume the role of a character of a book by providing old costumes for them to wear during the time they are reading the book or having it read to them. By being allowed to wear costumes, children become a part of the plot and the time. If two children are reading a story at the same time, they can assume particular roles and develop their own story lines. To capitalize on their interests, the caregiver should encourage children to write and illustrate or act on their own interpretations.

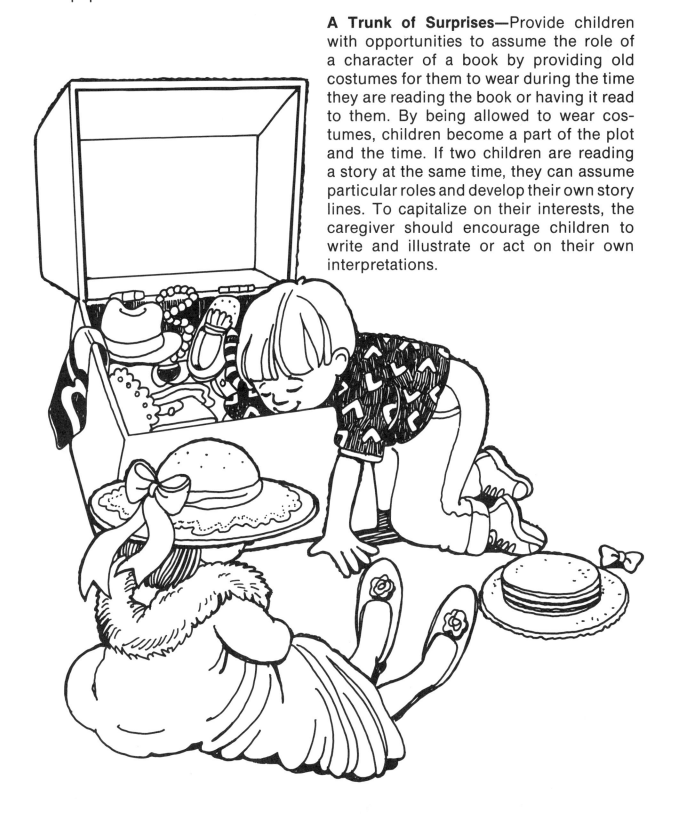

GA1335

Publisher's Corner—Encourage children to become their own publishers of books. All that is needed is construction paper, a hole punch, brads, crayons or paints and special times when the caregiver can provide direct assistance.

Children can be instructed to use what they found interesting from their reading to create or re-create books of their own. Cooperative efforts will yield more language production. Specific tasks can be assigned and completed. For instance, one child may wish to illustrate a story while another may choose to write, dictate or record the dialogue. As the children prepare for their books, having conferences with the teacher for suggestions and assistance will be beneficial. The end result is books of their own to be displayed and placed on the shelves with others found in the classroom.

If the teacher wants children to prepare their books independently or if this is a choice that children make on their own, then a rebus chart showing the steps in book preparation should be placed in the Publisher's Corner.

Reading one another's publications will occur if the child-made books are placed in the Book Corner. Special sharing times should be scheduled so that individual children can read their books to others in the class or to a small group.

If possible, sharing the books with other classes of children will extend children's learning.

Steps

1.) Write a story (or several).

2.) Collect and paint or draw a cover (or use poster board).

3.) Put a title on your cover.

4.) Bind together with brads, yarn, staples, rings, or spiral binding.

5.) Place in the Book Corner for others to read.

Note of Interest: When it comes time for the children to share their efforts with their parents, the caregiver can make a Xerox copy for each child involved and keep the original in the class library. Or a checkout procedure can be developed so that children can take published books home on occasion.

GA1335

Book Puzzles—Purchase as many paper versions of the books that are in the Book Corner and carefully separate the pages with a paper cutter. Laminate the individual pages so that these materials may be used over and over again for a number of years. Mix up the pages and put them in an envelope in the Book Corner. The challenge for children is to place the pages in the correct order based on their memory of the story pictures and print. If this procedure is too difficult for prekindergartners, ask them to match the pictures to the copy of the book.

Sentence Strips—Using the Book Puzzles described above, prepare sentence strips which match the print on each of the book's pages. After children have had positive experiences with the Book Puzzles, place the sentence strips in the envelopes with the book so that children can match the print on the strips to the print on the pages. When children have had many experiences with the sentence strips, challenge them to put the strips in order without the visual cues provided by the pictures in the book. This latter procedure might be better as a whole-group experience (with the use of a pocket chart). For first and second graders, the activity could become more difficult by using more difficult reading material.

Book Corner Bathtub—Bring in an old bathtub (one with pedestal feet is preferable) to use in the Book Corner as a comfortable place for children to read. Fill it with many large pillows and a teddy bear or other stuffed animals. Make sure that the lighting is appropriate for reading purposes.

GA1335

Books for the Book Corner:

Ahlberg, Janet, and Allan Ahlberg. *Each Peach, Pear, Plum.* Penguin Books, 1986.

Allen, Pamela. *I Wish I Had a Pirate Suit.* New York: Viking, 1990.

Asch, Frank. *Goodbye House.* Englewood Cliffs, New Jersey: Prentice Hall, 1986.

Brown, Margaret Wise. *Runaway Bunny.* New York: Harper and Row, 1977.

Cherry, Lynne. *Archie, Follow Me.* New York: Dutton, 1990.

Dubanevich, Arlene. *Tom's Tail.* New York: Viking, 1990.

Eastman, Philip D. *Go, Dog, Go!* New York: Random House, 1966.

Erlich, Amy. *Cinderella.* New York: Dial, 1990.

_____ . *Leo, Zack, and Emmie Together Again.* New York: Dial, 1990.

Flack, Marjorie. *The Story About Ping.* New York: Viking, 1977.

Gag, Wanda. *Millions of Cats.* New York: Putnam, 1988.

Gullikson, Sandy. *Trouble for Breakfast.* New York: Dial, 1990.

Hale, Kathleen. *Orlando Keeps a Cat.* New York: Puffin, 1990.

_____ . *Orlando the Marmalade Cat: A Camping Holiday.* New York: Puffin, 1990.

Harmer, Julie. *Prayers for Children.* New York: Viking, 1990.

Haviland, Virginia. *The Fairy Tale Treasury.* New York: Dell, 1986.

Hoban, Russell. *Bedtime for Frances.* New York: Harper and Row, 1976.

Kalman, Maria. *Hey Willie, See the Pyramids.* New York: Puffin, 1990.

_____ . *Max Makes a Million.* New York: Puffin, 1990.

Hennessy, B.G. *Eeney Meeney Miney Mo.* New York: Viking, 1990.

King, Larry. *Because of Lozo Brown.* New York: Puffin, 1990.

Levine, Abby. *You Push, I Ride.* New York: Puffin, 1990.

GA1335

Lindhbergh, Reeve. *The Day the Goose Got Loose.* New York: Dell, 1990.

Low, Alice. *Zena and the Witch Circus.* New York: Dial, 1990.

McPhail, David. *Pig Pig Gets a Job.* New York: Dutton, 1990.

Marshall, James. *Hansel and Gretel.* New York: Dial, 1990.

Milne, A. A. *The House at Pooh Corner.* New York: Dell, 1988.

Minarik, Eloa Halmelund. *Percy and the Five Houses.* New York: Puffin, 1990.

Pryor, Ainslie. *The Baby Blue Cat and the Smiley Worm Doll.* New York: Viking, 1990.

Ross, Tony. *Stone Soup.* New York: Dial, 1990.

Schindler, Regine. *The Bear's Cave.* New York: Dial, 1990.

Sendak, Maurice. *Nutshell Library.* New York: Harper and Row, 1977.

_____. *Where the Wild Things Are.* New York: Harper and Row, 1988.

Slobodkina, Esphry. *Caps for Sale.* New York: Harper and Row, 1987.

Viorst, Judith. *Alexander and the Terrible, Horrible, No Good, Very Bad Day.* New York: Macmillan, 1987.

Wickstrom, Sylvie. *Turkey on the Loose!* New York: Dial, 1990.

Wild, Jocelyn. *Florence and Eric Take the Cake.* New York: Dial, 1990.

GA1335

Puppet Center

Puppets hold a special appeal for children, and wise teachers use them in a variety of ways in the classroom to add zest and pleasure to classroom activity. The Puppet Center provides students with an opportunity for creative expression and to associate particular actions with details in a story or a poem. Children find the value in taking on the role of another character which they can control. The characterizations children depict rely on the rich literature experiences they have had in the classroom. If children know "The Three Billy Goats Gruff" story and puppets resembling goats are in the Puppet Center, then children want to reenact the story. Story retellings are important for the development of verbalizations of interesting language, sequential skills, perseverance to a task, experimentation with vocalizations, and interactions with other children's roles. For shy or insecure children, puppetry promotes communication skills because they are able to assume the role of a character in a nonthreatening setting. Children even enjoy making their own puppets!

The purposes of the Puppet Center are as follows:

To assist children in verbalizing the rich cultural heritage of literature they have enjoyed in the classroom

To create a situation where children are learning about story grammar and story sequence

To allow children an opportunity to use their voices to portray literary characters they know about

To provide children with an avenue of self-expression in making up their own puppet stories and plays

To give children further decision-making opportunities in determining how roles will be played and who will play each part

To help children interact socially through a play setting which has very serious elements to it

Here's what you need to prepare a Puppet Center.

Puppet theater or stage (this could be made by a parent volunteer or it could be a make-shift stage constructed out of a sheet draped over a dowel rod)

Storage space to hold commercial, teacher-made, and child-made puppets

Materials which children can use to make their own puppets (these could possibly be housed in the Art Center): paper plates, tongue depressors, Popsicle sticks, pipe cleaners, cotton balls, rickrack, yarn, old socks, fabric scraps, paper sacks, construction paper, buttons, sequins, beads, ribbons, purchased eyes, glue or glue stick, large needles and thread, Styrofoam balls (all sizes) and cups, and other miscellaneous items

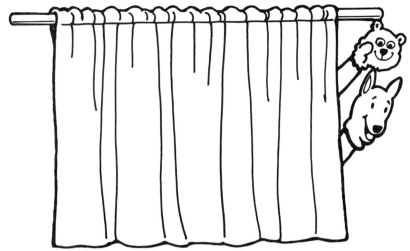

A typical floor plan for the Puppet Center might look like the following:

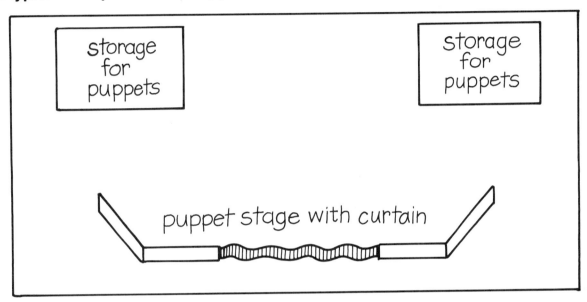

storage for puppets

storage for puppets

puppet stage with curtain

Here are some ideas to try to enhance language learning.

Box Office Bonanza—Set up a small table and chairs near the Puppet Center so that children can make "theater" tickets to sell and handbills to advertise an upcoming show in the Center. Provide writing supplies of all types—construction paper, poster board, pencils, markers, printer's set, ink pad, butcher paper, etc.— so that writing will occur. When a puppet presentation is organized, role-play selling the tickets for the big show.

The Show Does Go On!—When a group of children have a puppet show to present, use written signs to inform other children in the class about the specifics of the show. Examples of information which could be shared are

    what time the show will be performed
    where to pick up tickets
    which seats are reserved
    which act is being presented
    how much time is available for intermission
    if refreshments are available and how much they cost

Another writing activity is to prepare a program which lists the characters and the roles they play.

GA1335

A Trip to Remember

The caregiver can read the following story using puppets to provide the appropriate actions. The story is designed to demonstrate how the center can be used and the advantage of learning to read.

Zelma was a small child from the planet Velcroy. She lived there with her parents and small pet elpot named Ibu. Now Ibu was a strange creature indeed, looking something like a purple dog with wings. Not only could Ibu walk, he could fly as well—which is well and good as long as he stayed outside. But on those cold days when he was brought inside, Zelma and Ibu could drive her parents crazy.

One day, Zelma decided to take a short trip in her own spaceship to the planet Earth and visit a children's museum there. Her parents told her the trip was fine as long as she was home before dark. She was allowed to take Ibu with her only after she promised to keep him on his leash.

Now Zelma looked almost like children on earth except she had orange hair and her skin was green. It was lucky for her that she landed her ship in a play area where there were only children, because differences in people don't bother children too much.

After Zelma and Ibu landed their ship, they started walking toward the play area. The first people they met were Brittany and Chad, who were playing in the sandbox. When Chad and Brittany saw Zelma and Ibu, they were a little afraid, but not too much since Zelma was a child like they were and Ibu was on a leash. Still, they were prepared to run like the wind if Zelma and Ibu were not nice.

As it turned out, they all became friends and Chad wanted to know what kind of glue Zelma used on Ibu to make those wings stick. But once Ibu flew, he knew those wings were for real. Both he and Brittany thought Ibu was the neatest pet they had ever seen.

After they all played for a while, Zelma said she would like to go to the children's museum. Brittany and Chad told Zelma they would be glad to take her there. On their walk, they came to a stop sign and Zelma and Ibu didn't stop. Luckily, Brittany was able to call Zelma back to the corner before she was hit by a car.

"How did you know to stop?" asked Zelma.

"Because the sign says so," Chad replied. Chad then pointed to the stop sign and read it to Zelma.

"I still don't understand," she said. "It just looks like a bunch of crooked paint to me. On our planet, we do not have letters or words. We learn everything from our parents. Why do you have these letters or need to do what you call, read?"

"Because reading helps us to learn when there are no parents around," replied Brittany. "Besides, our parents work and can't be with us all of the time."

"Yeah, our teachers tell us that learning to read can help us to learn whether we are at school, home, play or anywhere," added Chad. "Reading street and road signs will help us find our way to the museum."

By this time Zelma was very curious about reading and wanted to learn more about these strange shapes. Lucky for her, Chad and Brittany were good teachers.

Once they arrived at the museum, Brittany took Zelma to an airplane display. There, she told her about the planes and how people used to fly them.

"How do you know so much about these flying objects?" questioned Zelma.

"It's easy. I just read the information on each of these displays," Brittany replied.

"This reading must be a lot of fun. My parents teach me a lot of things, but I could learn even more if I could read," Zelma noted.

For the rest of the afternoon, Chad and Brittany showed Zelma and Ibu all sorts of neat things in the museum and read all of the information on all of the displays. The truth is, Chad and Brittany were pretty proud they could read and share all of this information with their new friends.

Pretty soon it started getting late and Zelma and Ibu had to return home. Zelma was very excited about this thing the earth children called reading, and she wanted to learn more. So, on the way back to the spaceship, Chad and Brittany stopped by their homes and gave some of their books to Zelma to take back to Velcroy with her.

"I know it will take a lot of work, but I am going to learn to read when I get home," Zelma said. "The books you gave me will be very useful. But what happens when I want to teach my other friends to read and I run out of books?"

"That's easy," said Chad. "You can write your own books."

"What a great idea!" exclaimed Zelma. And with that she and Ibu returned home.

Follow-up questions:
    What books would you give Zelma to take with her?
    Why do you think that it is sometimes hard to learn to read?

GA1335

The teacher might use one of the following puppet variations to create characters for "A Trip to Remember":

Zelma

Ibu

Brittany

Chad

34

"A Trip to Remember" Flannel Board Story—Teachers could adapt the story "A Trip to Remember" for flannel board by using the following patterns:

GA1335

Letter Home to Mom—Guide children in writing a letter home to parents asking for materials to include in the Puppet Construction Area. The letter writing activity could be a whole-group experience with all children contributing to its construction. The teacher could type, copy and send it home.

September 17, 1991

Dear Mom:

We are starting a Puppet Center at school. Please help us by sending some of these things:

buttons	old socks
pipe cleaners	scrap material
rickrack	felt squares
Styrofoam cups	paper plates
glitter	sequins
Popsicle sticks	Styrofoam worms
tongue depressors	yarn
ribbon	Styrofoam balls
paper sacks	egg cartons

Thank you for helping us.

Mrs. Sandoval's Class

Puppet Construction Area—After the letter is taken home and materials begin to arrive, set them aside on a table near the Puppet Center or in the Art Center for children to use to construct their own puppets. Children can be very creative if they are given the opportunity. The teacher can talk to children about features of specific storybook characters to develop an interest in making puppets, but showing them a model to follow will defeat the creative purpose of this activity.

Once the puppets are completed, allow children to use them in the Puppet Center. The teacher could capture some of their stories on tape or snap photographs of their puppet creations to send home or to include in a record of the year which will be shared at an end-of-the-school-year function.

Cassette Staging—Allow the children to use the puppets or masks to act out simple stories, either real or imaginary, while a cassette recording may be used or another child can read while the actions take place. Learning the association of words and actions will be important for the child who has had little experience with storytelling.

Children can also use their puppets in other areas of the classroom: in the dollhouse, the Housekeeping Center, the Book Corner, or in the Art Center where the puppets could become people to accompany box sculptures children have made.

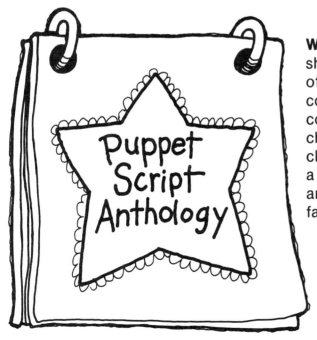

Writing Puppet Scripts—Older children should begin to write their scripts as part of the writing process. If the teacher collects them into an anthology, the scripts could be shared with other classrooms of children or placed in the Book Corner for classmates to read. Children should gain a great deal of pride in checking out the anthology to take home to share with their families.

GA1335

Grocery Store Center

The Grocery Store Center has long been a popular center with young children. Because families go together to the grocery store, the natural step is to set up a Grocery Store Center so that children can practice what they observe in real life. Even families who use a large amount of fast food items make occasional trips to the grocery store to purchase milk, bread, and other staples.

The Grocery Store Center is a natural place for children to make connection with print. Youngsters have been "reading" cereal boxes, candy bar and gum wrappers, and other commercial packaging for years. From about the age of two, children can recognize their favorite food items by the box and wrapper labels. What most adults fail to understand is that this is reading. Emphasizing to children that they are reading when they are able to select Cheerios instead of Trix is a step toward reading acquisition.

The purposes of the Grocery Store Center are as follows:

To expose children to elementary marketing techniques

To provide opportunities for children to read print through the use of packaging which is meaningful and relevant to them

To give children experiences with numbers and money

To model the behaviors of grocery store personnel to play roles

To help children to use writing as they prepare "specials sheets," grocery lists, signs and receipts in the Grocery Store Center

Here's what you need to plan a Grocery Store Center.

Table or box to serve as a checkout counter

Toy cash register which works

Shelves to stock empty product containers

Empty product containers of all types

Large enough space to plan for grocery store departments (produce, meat market, bakery, dairy section, etc.)

Banners and posters commonly seen in grocery stores (many are willing to give these away when they are discarded if teachers will request them)

Miniature grocery store cart or basket

Paper sacks, pencils and paper, cash register tape, note or statement pads

Stock person's apron and cap or white jacket

GA1335

A typical Grocery Store Center floor plan might look like the following:

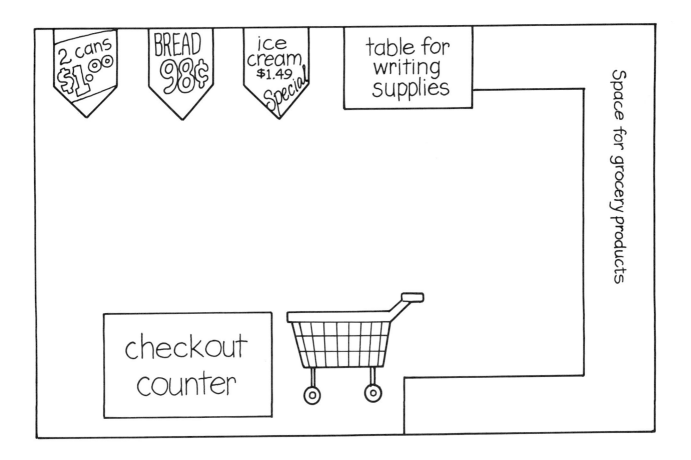

Determining Cost—An extremely difficult concept to teach students is the relative costs of products. To assist in this area, the caregiver should stock the grocery center shelves with the most commonly used items by children (representing the major food groups and a few other frequently used products). Such things as milk, fruit, basic cereals, toothpaste, canned vegetables, etc., should be prominently displayed on the shelves. On a piece of poster board hanging behind the writing supplies, the caretaker should have pictorial comparisons of relative costs. For instance, a gallon of milk may cost as much as a whole chicken which is about the same as two tubes of toothpaste or twelve peaches or one pound of candy. With these sorts of examples being provided, children can begin to develop an understanding why it is not always possible to buy every item they would like, especially if there is a budget involved. Small groups of children should be encouraged to talk to each other about the things they buy in the grocery store and about some items they would like to buy but often cost too much.

Shop, Shop, Shop—Grocery ads should be included in the table containing writing supplies so that children can create lists of things to buy from these ads. If children are able to write, they can write the names of the products and the corresponding prices. Should children be unable to write, they can cut out the pictures and prices of the products from the advertisements. A certain amount of play money or tokens representing money could be given to each child based on his/her family size. Colors could be used to denote relative value. For instance, on a story price chart, the color yellow could buy one chicken, one gallon of milk, six cans of corn, etc., while a blue token could buy three cans of corn, one tube of toothpaste, etc.

Once the basic procedures have been established, the child is ready to shop. Also, a grocery worker is prepared to assist in locating certain products while another could be ready to check the individual out, take the money and bag the purchases. In addition, courtesy should be stressed at all times as a form of modeling for actual shopping trips. When the items have been purchased and bagged, each child should assist in returning the goods to the appropriate locations in the store and putting the equipment away. Then the roles could be changed if the interest level is still high.

Preparing for the Sale—Have the children create their own ads based on the grocery ads found on the writing table. A small group should collectively decide what they should put on sale, how it should be displayed and the amount of money they should charge. Manila paper can be used, and ads could be developed which are similar to those found in the papers each week. Once this activity is completed, the children can use this information to "Shop, Shop, Shop!"

Be Prepared—Ask the students to buy a list of groceries of their choosing with the understanding that they would have to explain why they bought certain items to their parents (another child in the small group). This activity could provide practice in basic decision making. Further, the role reversal could help children understand some of the reasons parents make the decisions they do regarding product purchases.

Product Identification—Several product containers could be used to assist the children in helping to identify what is inside. The names of the products could be covered and the children could guess what is in the container. They should share what clues they used to make their predictions.

Once this activity has been completed, the container could be covered with the exception of the product name, and the children could guess what is inside.

Is What I See What I Get?—Children are occasionally misled by product packaging. In other words, what they see on the outside is not always what is found on the inside. Several relatively inexpensive products with inviting pictures could be purchased and the actual contents could be compared with what is actually inside (either in large or small group discussion). The teacher could record the reported differences and help the children summarize what they think they should tell their parents about what they learned.

Developing a discussion about the propaganda devices advertisers use to sell their products could be an extension of this activity.

A Book for the Grocery Store Center:

Gretz, Susanna. *Teddy Bears Go Shopping.* New York: Four Winds Press, 1982.

Science Center

Children love science much more than teachers realize! Finding the last flower in spring, bringing a fuzzy caterpillar into the classroom, enjoying a cold winter's day, finding out how rain falls, experimenting with water, using magnets for the first time—all of these experiences are invaluable to children as a foundation for later science experiences. The Science Center is a logical way to bring some of the outside world indoors.

Science helps develop analytical thinking. It helps children discover the solutions to problems they encounter in their environment. It promotes a sense of competence in children when they understand the causes of specific events and natural phenomena. Though not immediately apparent, science correlates well with language development. Scientists keep records, and to use the Science Center to its fullest, children must also keep records. Amateur scientists discover a relevant need for print!

The purposes of the Science Center are as follows:

To introduce children to the methods of the scientist and the scientific process

To allow sensory experiences with all types of natural and man-made artifacts

To assist children in discovering cause and effect relationships through various experiments

To challenge children to develop problem-solving techniques and thinking skills individually and in groups

To acquire the skill of choosing specific data to collect and collecting it

To learn how to record scientific data which is collected at the Science Center

Here's what you need to prepare a Science Center.

One rectangular table near a source of light (a classroom window is preferable)

Many plants and a watering can

Books with scientific information in them (many beautiful publications are currently available)

Scientific equipment designed for young children—examples are magnets, magnifying glasses, microscopes, balance scales, petri dishes, rules, storage boxes, jars (plastic varieties are safer)

Classroom animals and cages (if permissible) and food for them

Ant farm

Charts and markers (for recording collecting data)

A typical floor plan for the Science Center might look like the following:

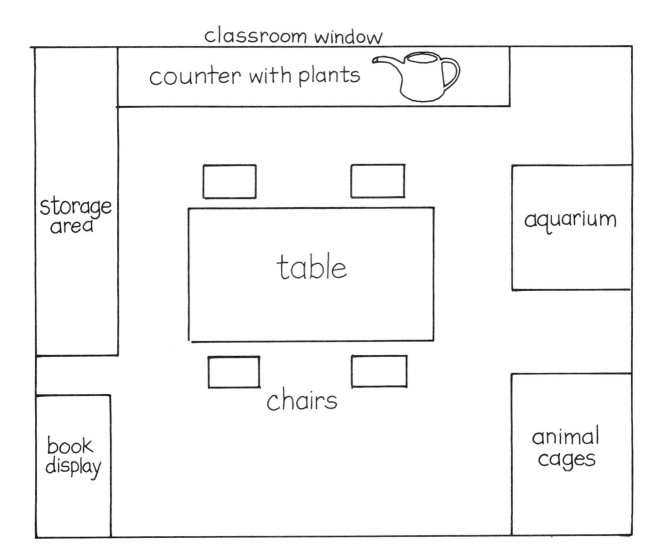

Here are some ideas to try to enhance language learning.

Garden Corner—This area of the center should be located near windows, since the children will be attempting to grow seeds. Though this is not a segment of the center that will be used every day, children will want to check on the progress of their particular plant projects on a regular basis.

43

GA1335

Children are capable of learning about the proper care necessary to keep plants alive. An excellent way to introduce the proper care for plants is by allowing children to plant seeds in Styrofoam cups and to provide them with the necessary sunlight and water over a period of time to see if they grow. Learning more about plants prior to the actual planting of the seeds is a step toward literacy and investigating information in books, models, scientific data collection and research skills.

Once the children have learned about planting and care, each is to label a cup, fill with soil and plant a lima bean seed. A schedule for watering will be established and the children will await the time when the seeds actually grow. For those children who may not be successful, a second bean can be planted. The children will both be predicting what will happen when the plant grows and recording the results of their efforts.

Another way to record the growth of plants is to take Polaroid photographs regularly and glue them onto a chart and let children dictate statements about the changes.

Usually early childhood classrooms have plants in them for their aesthetic value, and the teacher should let the children assist in their care. Also, the children can use their measuring devices from the Manipulatives Center to keep a record of how the plants are growing.

Thar' She Blows—This section of the learning center is for children to learn more about volcanoes. An outstanding motivation for this particular table is a papier-mâché volcano sitting in the middle of the table. It should be small and colorful. Where the hole in the top of the volcano is located, the teacher should place an inverted small metal lid (like those found on the top of a cooking oil container) disguised by the papier-mâché itself.

The center should contain books and pictures of volcanoes, lava rocks and possibly a filmstrip or video tape (if available). Even though it is not appropriate to attempt to teach mapping skills, a globe can be labeled where active volcanoes are found. The children can then proceed to learn as much as they can about these natural occurrences.

As an application of their experiences, pictures can be drawn and colored and stories written and/or told. When the children complete all of the required assignments, then they can cause a volcano eruption. The teacher allows a child to place one teaspoon of magic white powder (baking soda) in the top of the volcano and carefully add a mysterious red liquid (vinegar with red food coloring). The results are a simulated and safe eruption. Afterward, the children should take paper towels and clean up the "lava." The procedure can be repeated for the next set of children working in the center.

volcano

by Kim Lee

44

GA1335

Junior Scientists

Try some of the following ideas which will allow children to experiment with materials and make some assumptions about why objects work as they do.

They All Fall Down—Provide a softball, marble, small Styrofoam ball, and a tennis ball on a table in the Science Center. Ask children to drop two balls at the same time and record the results. The objects should be dropped from the same height simultaneously.

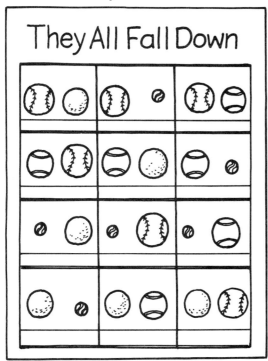

Younger children will need to have the chart prepared by the teacher, but older children can prepare their own. Divide the chart into two columns showing all the possible pairings of balls (softball and tennis ball; softball and marble; softball and Styrofoam ball; and Styrofoam ball and marble). For readers, the written words are sufficient, but pictures will be needed for nonreaders. Tell children that each experiment should be done at least three times (in the true nature of science).

If done properly, the objects will hit the ground at the same time. How and why does this happen? Junior scientists can find out through reading about gravity or having the reasons played to them using a cassette tape recording.

How Much Does It Take?—Provide a simple set of balance scales and several different objects to weigh. Suggestions are an empty box, a box of marbles, a container of sand, a container of water, a container of paper clips, a container of noodles, a container of erasers, and any other objects which can be easily weighed. When possible, all of the containers holding the objects should be the same size and dimensions.

The purpose of these exercises is to introduce children to the concept of mass. For instance, a container of noodles will weigh less than an identical container of sand, a container of erasers less than a container of water, and an empty box less than the container of noodles. Provide a chart (or children can prepare their own) and allow children to experiment with the different combinations and record their results. The scientific question is: If all containers are the same size, why don't they weigh the same? The junior scientists will want to know.

GA1335

How Does It Do That?—Collect the following items for the Science Center table: freezer bags that seal, several Alka Seltzer tablets, carbonated water (clear, soft drink is sufficient), lima bean seeds, an inflated balloon placed on the top of a plastic soft-drink bottle, a container filled with ice, a container filled with water, baking soda, vinegar, small birthday candles, a quart-sized plastic jar, a small glass or plastic container and a pencil. Ask the junior scientists to work in pairs or small groups to answer the following scientific questions which could be given orally or prepared on sentence strips (for second graders).

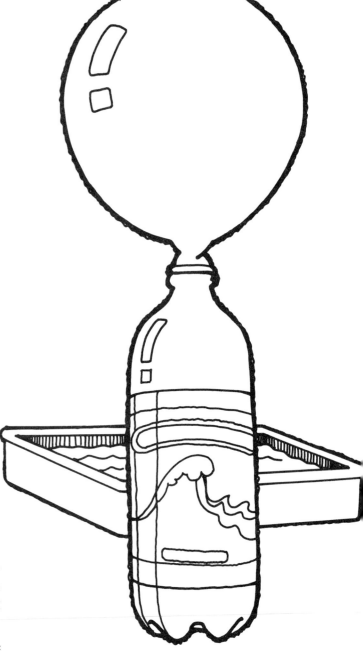

Question: What happens if a freezer bag is half-filled with water, two Alka Seltzer tablets are added and the bag is sealed?

Answer: The freezer bag will expand and become larger.

Question: What happens if lima bean seeds are placed in a container of carbonated water?

Answer: The carbonated water will make the seeds appear to "dance" from the bottom to top.

Question: What happens if a tablespoon of baking soda is placed in a small container of vinegar?

Answer: There will be foam.

Question: What happens to a pencil when it is placed in a glass of water?

Answer: The pencil appears to be broken because of the effect of light on the water.

Question: What happens if the inflated balloon on the plastic soft-drink bottle (this step completed by the teacher) is placed in a pan of ice water?*

Answer: The balloon will get smaller.

Question: What will happen if a candle (to be lit by the teacher and safety precautions provided) is covered by a container (quart jar)?*

Answer: The flame will go out because of the lack of oxygen.

*This will need to be supervised carefully by the teacher or adult volunteer.

Two sources for helping children to find the answers to these questions are *Childcraft* and Walt Disney's *My First Encyclopedia Set* (Grolier Enterprises).

What Sticks and What Doesn't?—Place a variety of magnets on a small table in the center including circle magnets, bar magnets, horseshoe magnets and any others which are available. Include objects that are or are not attracted by magnets (paper clips, nails, aluminum objects, shavings, small wooden and rubber objects, corks, etc.). Using a "junior scientist" check sheet, the children should test each of the objects to see whether or not they are attracted to the magnets and record the results.

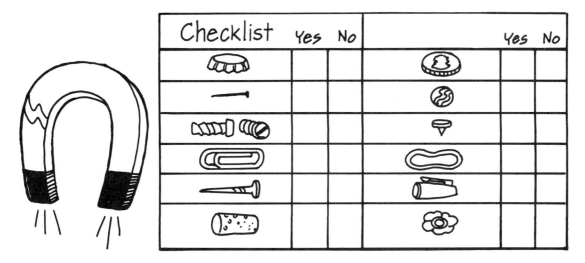

In an adjacent area, the teacher should take another set of magnets and attach them to several sheets of tagboard (securing the board on the table with masking tape should be adequate). Using metal filings, the small groups of children will sprinkle them over the tagboard with the magnets and observe the patterns which result. Ask the children to illustrate their observations. For maximum effectiveness, the teacher should attach magnets to the tagboard with like poles pointing toward each other and opposite poles pointing toward each other.

How does all of this work? The junior scientists need to investigate to find out why.

Only the Shadow Knows—For this activity, the caregiver will need flashlights, several cutout or plastic figures and a white wall of projection. Pose the following questions:

What happens if a child places a plastic toy between him or her and the white wall and shines a light on the figure?
(There is a shadow.)

What happens to the shadow if the figure is moved closer to the light?
(The shadow is larger.)

What happens to the shadow if the figure is moved away from the light?
(The shadow is smaller.)

What happens if a child holds up a paper figure, shines a light on it and blows air on it?
(The shadow will move.)

Ask the children to create shadows of their own.

GA1335

Dinosaur Cave—Children's unending fascination with dinosaurs begins very early in their lives. To take advantage of these interests, the teacher can create a cave in one corner of the learning center. A simple, dark curtain or sheet can be used to establish the entrance and body of the cave. Since light is necessary, the cave should probably have open sides. Stock one corner with all sorts of dinosaur books, plus a small reading lamp. The colorful pictures and interesting facts will make this extremely interesting reading. If the students are nonreaders, the teacher can provide cassette recordings of the stories.

In another section of the cave, the teacher can have objects that represent odd dinosaur facts. For instance, a six-inch (15.24 cm) ruler or stick can be used to demonstrate the length of a Tyrannosaurus rex tooth, a golf ball to represent the size of the Stegosaurus brain, etc. The caregiver can challenge the children to come up with other odd facts about dinosaurs and find their own representations of these facts.

Dinosaur Masks—Children can make dinosaur masks using a section of poster board, paints or crayons and a tongue depressor. Each child can make the face of his/her favorite dinosaur and glue it on the stick for display. Should time and the opportunity present itself, the children as a group can give clues about the dinosaurs represented on their masks and see if the other children can guess which one it is.

Later, use the dinosaur masks in the Puppet Center to create a play about dinosaurs.

49

GA1335

Books for the Science Center:

Berenstain, Stan and Jan. *The Day of the Dinosaur.* New York: Random House, 1987.

Bjork, Christina. *Linnea's Windowsill Garden.* Stockholm: Raben & Sjogren, 1988.

Branley, Franklyn M. *The Beginning of the Earth.* New York: Harper and Row, 1988.

_____ . *The Big Dipper.* New York: Crowell Company, 1962.

_____ . *The Planets in Our Solar System.* New York: Crowell Junior Books, 1981.

_____ . *Saturn: The Spectacular Planet.* New York: Crowell Junior Books, 1983.

_____ . *The Sun; Our Nearest Star.* New York: Crowell Co., 1961.

Briggs, Raymond. *The Snowman.* New York: Random House, 1986.

Carle, Eric. *The Very Busy Spider.* New York: Philomel Books, 1989.

Graham, Thomas. *Mr. Bear's Chair.* New York: Dutton, 1990.

Hirschi, Ron. *Spring.* New York: Cobblehill, 1990.

_____ . *Winter.* New York: Cobblehill, 1990.

King, Elizabeth. *The Pumpkin Patch.* New York: Dutton, 1990.

Lauber, Patricia. *Dinosaurs Walked Here.* New York: Bradbury Press, 1987.

_____ . *The News About Dinosaurs.* New York: Bradbury Press, 1989.

_____ . *Snakes Are Hunters.* New York: Harper and Row, 1988.

_____ . *Volcano.* New York: Bradbury Press, 1986.

Schweninger, Ann. *Wintertime,* New York: Viking, 1990.

Selsam, Millicent E. *Egg to Chicken.* New York: Harper and Row, 1987.

_____ . *A First Look at Caterpillars.* New York: Walker & Co., 1987.

_____ . *A First Look at Rocks.* New York: Walker & Co., 1984.

_____ . *A First Look at Sea Shells.* New York: Walker & Co., 1983.

_____ . *A First Look at Whales.* New York: Walker & Co., 1980.

GA1335

_____ . *A First Look at the World of Plants.* New York: Walker & Co., 1978.

_____ . *How Kittens Grow.* New York: Four Winds Press, 1977.

_____ . *How Puppies Grow.* New York: Four Winds Press, 1977.

_____ . *Is This a Baby Dinosaur?* New York: Harper and Row, 1984.

Simon, Seymour. *Earth: Our Planet in Space.* New York: Four Winds Press, 1984.

_____ . *Jupiter.* New York: William Morrow & Company, 1985.

_____ . *The Long Journey from Space.* New York: Crown.

_____ . *The Moon.* New York: Four Winds Press, 1984.

_____ . *The Smallest Dinosaur.* New York: Crown, 1987.

_____ . *Stars.* New York: William Morrow & Company, 1986.

_____ . *The Sun.* New York: William Morrow & Company, 1986.

_____ . *Uranus.* New York: William Morrow & Company, 1987.

Titherginton, Jeanne. *Pumpkin, Pumpkin.* New York: Scholastic, Inc., 1986.

Weiss, Nicki. *Where Does the Brown Bear Go?* New York: Puffin, 1990.

Wellington, Monica. *Seasons of Swans.* New York: Dutton, 1990.

GA1335

Part II
Special Topical Centers

Special Topical Centers

Themes of study change on a regular basis in early childhood classrooms in order to accommodate children's ever-broadening interests in their environment and in one another. As a consequence, teachers need areas of the classroom which they can use to capitalize on the natural curiosity young children have to learn. Often adults plan units of study for their children, but these plans are affected by current events and by children's contributions to on-going classroom activity.

Topics of study should be relevant to young children. When instruction does not relate to children's lives, then children are not as interested in it. Focusing instead on content areas which are familiar to children will yield better results. Of course, preparing a center to accompany the theme provides an opportunity for children to experience first-hand the artifacts and natural paraphernalia related to the subject. The Special Topical Center supports the presentation of content which might otherwise seem ordinary to children.

Tips for Setting Up Special Centers:

1. Place objects and materials in the center which children can use. Hands-on experiences are essential to young children because of the sensory learning which is inherent in them.

2. The center should be attractive, but not too beautiful. Preparing a center which seems to have a "Do not touch" sign on it will not produce the expected learning. Aesthetics has a place in the early childhood classroom, but not at the expense of children using materials and equipment.

3. Allow space for children to bring their own contributions from home. Using this procedure provides another aspect of relevancy to the study, because children feel involved in their learning if they are making contributions.

4. Formalize a procedure for allowing children to play in and use the center. Some of the procedures suggested in Part I could be appropriate here.

Nursery Rhymes Center

Nursery rhymes are an excellent approach to encouraging language acquisition. The rhythm of the rhymes, the rhyme of the poetry, the introduction of interesting characters and problems in nursery rhymes have made them perennial favorites. Many a young parent and young teacher are amazed at their own pleasure when they renew their acquaintances with Little Miss Muffet, Humpty Dumpty, Little Jack Horner, and Jack and Jill. Nursery rhymes and nursery rhyme characters are lifelong friends, ones which we are glad to share with the next generation.

The purposes of the Nursery Rhymes Center are as follows:

To expose children to classical literature by introducing them to nursery rhyme characters

To assist children in learning the rhythm, alliteration, and rhymes of nursery rhymes

To allow fantasy and imagination to occur as these make-believe characters are introduced

To encourage role playing and dramatic play as children act out favorite nursery rhymes

Here's what you need to prepare a Nursery Rhymes Center.

Table to display nursery rhyme books

Chairs or large pillows for children to sit in while they enjoy the books

Bulletin board to display pictures of nursery rhyme characters and any pictures or writing children have done about the rhymes

Props to encourage dramatic play, such as:

candle and candlestick for "Jack Be Nimble"
large cardboard box to serve as a wall for "Humpty Dumpty"
haystack for "Little Boy Blue"
tub for "Rub-a-Dub-Dub"
large shoe for "There Was an Old Woman"
small stool, a bowl, and a plastic spider for "Little Miss Muffet"
crown, a scepter (made out of a paper towel roll, and a robe) for "Old King Cole"
assortment of collars, shoes, buckles, hats, bow ties, and other Victorian-type costumes for children to wear
pail for "Jack and Jill"
shepherd's staff for "Mary Had a Little Lamb"
miniature hoe or spade for "Mary, Mary, Quite Contrary"
space for dramatic play (or the classroom's circle area may be used)

GA1335

A typical floor plan for the Nursery Rhymes Center might look like the following:

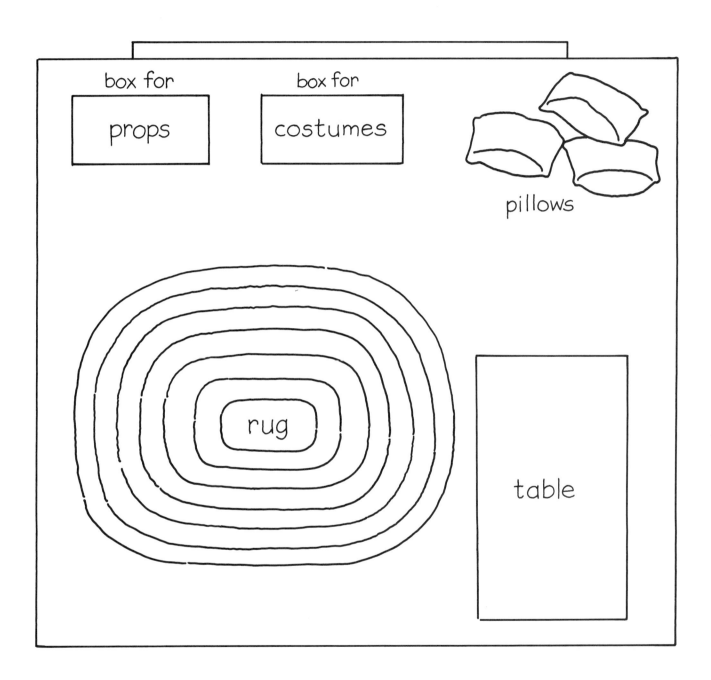

box for
props

box for
costumes

pillows

rug

table

Here are some ideas to try to enhance language learning.

Listening to Rhymes—Promote listening skills for younger children by preparing several cassette tapes of the rhymes being used and place them with the appropriate books and machines in the center close to the pillows. Read the nursery rhyme book during a large group time, giving special attention to the rhythm, alliteration, rhyme and other important features of the rhymes.

Then when children are in the Nursery Rhymes Center, two or three can choose a book and tape, turn the tape on and listen to each poem being read while attempting to follow along with the accompanying book. A simple cue (such as a bell) can be included at the appropriate time which indicates a page should be turned. Encourage the children to look and listen for other clues that would help them determine when it is time to turn the page.

After the children have been allowed to repeat this procedure several times (the number of times dependent on the children), encourage them to play a second tape of the poetry where there are no cues included. Through this process, the children will be able to discuss with the others in the group alternative methods of determining when a page should be turned. Since accuracy is not stressed, correctness or incorrectness should not be an issue. When the children are ready to share their accomplishments, the teacher should be a willing audience.

The teacher can also record (on the same cassette containing no cues) some of the favorite rhymes by reading a few lines and omitting a few words here and there. Have the children listen to the recording and predict what they think should come next. Depending on the age and maturational level of the children involved, one or several lines could be read prior to one or more being omitted. The children should be encouraged to take turns and provide cooperative support for each other. As a method of self-checking, the other tape of the nursery rhymes will be available.

 GA1335

Activity to Promote Comprehension—Encourage the children to feel free to use costumes and prop boxes to act out their favorite rhymes or characters in certain poems. They may choose to have a single child retell the story while they act out the parts, or they may choose to have several parts, depending on the poems being used. Should the caregiver choose to include puppets in the box for props, the children can use them to retell each rhyme. As an extension of this activity, encourage the children to change any portion they wish, mix and mesh characters and use dramatic play to demonstrate their interpretations. They can practice and perform on the rug area in the center.

Displaying Nursery Rhymes—Another excellent idea is to display well-known nursery rhymes on chart form. Then have flash cards to match words on the chart. As an example:

Humpty Dumpty sat on a wall; Humpty Dumpty had a great fall. All the King's horses And all the King's men Couldn't put Humpty Dumpty Together again.

Humpty
wall
fall
horses

After this experience, have the charts available with words missing. Children can then look for the missing words found on the flash cards. This activity should be quite beneficial for children at the end of the kindergarten year or at the beginning of first grade.

Nursery Rhyme Journals—Another way to encourage children to write is to ask them to keep a nursery rhyme journal. If several good nursery rhyme books are available, then children need to find the rhymes they like and copy the print onto a page of manila or newsprint paper (lined paper is appropriate for first or second graders, but unlined paper is better for younger children). These copies can be illustrated and bound together into a book if children want them in book form. Their copied selections can be "read" easily because children are so familiar with the rhymes that are their favorites.

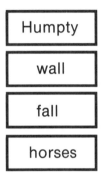

Hickory, dickory, dock,
The mouse ran up
the clock;
The clock struck one,
and down he came,
Hickory, dickory, dock.

Illustrating and Creating New Poems—Encourage children to work with partners to illustrate a rhyme that they create. They may want to write another rhyme about Little Boy Blue or Little Miss Muffet, for example, or they can create a completely new character. Of course, illustrations should also be included. Children can combine the evolving literacy skills they have in writing new nursery rhymes. The rhymes may be shared orally or at a later time, if children desire.

Old King Cole Word Wall—The teacher should tell the story in a group setting that Old King Cole has asked all of the children in the kingdom to help decorate the "wall" of his castle, which is a long sheet of butcher paper taped to a wall or tacked to a bulletin board. He specifically wants children to think of words which relate to all of the nursery rhymes they know. As children brainstorm their suggestions, the teacher should record their words. These will be useful later if children want to write stories about any of the characters. They can refer to the word wall to find the words they need to spell.

castle
wall
lamb
spider
bird
pocket

Leave space at the bottom of the wall so that children can add words to the list after the brainstorming session is over.

Old King Cole Word Bank—Once the word wall is complete, children can copy the words they select to put in their individual word banks (a collection of flash cards children can read which they keep independently). In a large group setting, the teacher can play a game to determine how well the children are reading their words. The teacher or another child can ask students to find a specific nursery rhyme character in their banks and display the cards to see. Keeping a checklist handy to check those who are recognizing the words correctly will facilitate a letter parent-teacher conference.

castle

Simply asking children to read the words they have in their banks is another easy technique to assess their reading ability.

Queen of Hearts Riddle Day—Assign each child the task of finding a prop or costume to represent a favorite nursery rhyme character and bring it to school on a predetermined day. Children can take turns guessing who each of their classmates is.

Older children may find that writing their own riddles for their props or costumes will be more challenging. If children have premarked their items with their names, then it will be easy to place the props and the written riddles on a table so that children with free time can browse and match the written riddle with its prop or costume.

Books for the Nursery Rhymes Center:

Ahlberg, Janet, and Allan Ahlberg. *Peek-A-Boo!* New York: Viking, 1990.

Arnold, Tedd, III. *Mother Goose's Words of Wit and Wisdom.* New York: Dial Books, 1990.

Bennett, Jill. *The Animal Fair.* New York: Viking, 1990.

Gilbert, Yvonne, III. *Baby's Book of Lullabies and Cradle Songs.* New York: Dial Books, 1990.

Hague, Michael, III. *Mother Goose: A Collection of Classic Nursery Rhymes.* New York: Holt, Rinehart and Winston, 1984.

Hoffmann, Hilde. *The City and Country Mother Goose.* New York: American Heritage Press, 1969.

Prelutsky, Jack. *Read-Aloud Rhymes for the Very Young.* New York: Alfred A. Knopf, 1986.

Tudor, Tasha, III. *Mother Goose.* New York: David McKay Company, Inc., 1972.

Wildsmith, Brian. *Mother Goose, A Collection of Nursery Rhymes.* New York: Franklin Watts, 1964.

Family Relationships Center

Children's families are important to them for very obvious reasons. Families represent security, and children learn about love and trust in their family relationships. Many educators recognize that parents are children's first teachers, and when children come to school, their interactions with other children have often been with siblings. Families influence who children will become and how they will behave socially, emotionally and intellectually in the larger society.

Studying family structures and children's roles in them is necessary for young children so that they can understand the likenesses and differences in families. Studying families can also provide children with other viewpoints about what families are and how they operate. This center is one that can be developed early in the year because of the nature of its theme. In the long run, it will probably be linked closely with the Housekeeping Center.

The purposes of the Family Relationships Center are as follows:

To help children understand the concept of family structure

To expose children to a variety of common family structures

To assist children in understanding that all family members have responsibilities within the family structure

To allow children to define what their family responsibilities are

To create opportunities for children to role-play family structures and situations

To give children the sense that being a member of a family is important because of physical and emotional reasons

Here's what you need to prepare a Family Relationships Center.

Bulletin board and pictures of a variety of family structures and ethnic groups

Table and several chairs

Magazines, picture books, and pictures of families

Dollhouse, dolls, and doll furniture

Child-sized rocking chair

Dolls (remember ethnic groups) and doll carriages

Large pillows, blankets, a cot (or mattress)

Large calendar which marks special holidays and children's birthdays

GA1335

A typical floor plan for the Family Relationships Center might look like the following:

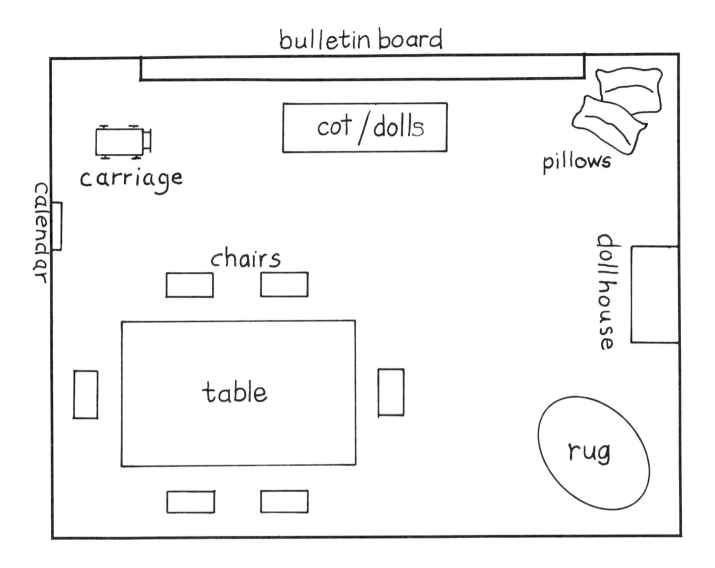

My Family Members—Provide magazines, construction paper, scissors and glue for the children. After the children have had opportunities to look through the magazines, ask them to pretend that they are making a picture of the individuals who take care of them. To complete the task they are to cut pictures out of magazines to represent each family member and glue them on construction paper. If the children are able to write or form letters, they can name the members of their families. Should the children prefer to draw pictures of their families instead of cutting pictures out of magazines, they should be permitted to do so. After completing this activity, the children can compare and contrast their family members to others in the class. This activity will vividly illustrate to the children in a nonjudgmental manner that most families are different.

Work Families Do—Most children come from households where both adults work or where the family is headed by a single adult. In both situations, each individual in the family will have certain responsibilities around the household. The message this activity is to transmit is that each effort will make a difference. To illustrate this, the children will be asked to complete a section of a mural on "How I Make a Difference in My Family." To complete this, each child will draw, color, paint or paste pictures of the many things he or she does around the house or other type of dwelling each day. The children should be encouraged to share that portion of the mural and to express verbally how each makes a difference around the household.

Special Days and Special Ways—The purpose of this activity is to assist children in the creation of a "Calendar of Special Days" involving their families. For those youngsters who may come from extremely large families, the list of special days may have to be restricted somewhat.

To complete this task, the teacher will need to supply a piece of wood for each child (approximately 8" x 11" [20.3 x 27.9 cm]) divided into nine squares (using magic marker). The caregiver will ask each child using this section of the center to take home a survey where the parents or guardians identify some of the major family days throughout the calendar year. Be sure that the survey contains both the month, date and event. The examples may range from family birthdays to formally recognized holidays. Should a parent or guardian not participate, the teacher can assist the child in developing a list of special days (which may or may not include holidays).

Once the lists have been returned, the teacher can assist the child in arranging the important family dates/events according to months, days and titles. If children are writing, they can develop each of the important date announcements with the information mentioned previously and glue on the board with one event per square. When these are completed, each child should have a calendar of special days throughout the year. When the glue and drawings have dried completely, a coat of clear varnish should be applied for gloss and permanence. The result will be a gift each parent or guardian will treasure for years.

What I Do to Help	What I Can Do Better

What I Can Do Better—Each child will need a piece of construction paper divided in two columns. One column should be labeled as "What I Do to Help" and the other "What I Can Do Better."

In preparation for this activity, the teacher can brainstorm with the children as a large group (or smaller if desired) the types of items to include. It is important that the ideas represented are practical and age appropriate. For instance, one thing children may do better is to tell the parents or guardians that they love them each day. Another area may be to remove their plates and glasses after a meal, or help make up a bed or make less noise when people are asleep. Basically, the list depends on the child.

Should the children be writers, the lists on the construction paper could be in pencil or crayon (with illustrations). If not, pictures could be drawn or cut out from magazines and the caregiver could assist in labeling (if necessary). Suggesting to children that drawing is a form of "writing" (their personal scripts) will help develop a sense of independence. The importance of this activity is that children realize they are an important part of their family and, as such, should think of others.

What My Family Likes—On poster board or other large paper used for paintings, each child should be encouraged to paint a picture of each family member. It would be useful if each member were painted in a separate section of the painting. The teacher can assist by dividing each page into the appropriate sections (one section per family member). When the paintings are completed, the child is to look through old magazines to find pictures which represent what each individual family member likes. This can include hobbies, sports, TV programs, books, food, cars and clothing. Should the children not know what certain family members like, encourage them to take an old magazine home with them (in case there are no reading materials available) and have a parent or guardian assist in identifying the things they like. After the children return to school with the pictures of the things the family member likes, they can glue them in the appropriate category on the picture.

Once the projects are completed, the teacher should encourage the children to put the pictures into a class book which can be checked out (as in a library) and taken home. This not only promotes verbal skills, but each child learns more about other children in the class. Further, it promotes discussions of similarities and differences in families.

64

Ways I Appreciate My Family—At this table, the children will be asked to create a picture to be presented to their immediate caregivers which expresses the many ways they appreciate their efforts. To complete the assignment, different colors of construction paper should be available for them to use. Then the child should identify three things his caregivers do that he/she appreciates. Should questions arise after sharing the ideas with a learning center partner, the teacher can provide assistance.

The actual pictures to be created should not be of people, but rather the different symbols that represent a caring environment. For instance, if the parent or guardian reads to the child, a picture of a book can be placed on the picture. If the child appreciates hugs and kisses, lips can be included to represent this effort. If it is cooking, a stove or a pan should be placed on the picture, etc. Since the pictures are to be made from and glued on construction paper, patterns are strictly optional. A highly appreciated message by the parents or guardians is when the pictures created by the children utilize the formula hugs and kisses + reading books + preparing meals = love (a picture of the traditional heart). Should the pictures created by the children be a little abstract, the adult can assist in labeling the actual actions that are appreciated. If children are writing, they can be requested to write a note of thanks to their parents or guardians to accompany the art when they take it home.

Family Album—Ask children to bring photographs of their families from home to place into a picture album titled "Our Families." A note explaining that these photographs will be returned when the Family Relationships topic discussion is complete should accompany children's requests for the pictures. When children bring their photographs, encourage them to label the family members' names to identify them in the picture album.

Days, Nights, and Weekends—Develop a small group discussion about routines and schedules which people have in their homes. Compare these schedules with those that children follow in school. Talking about what children do at school in relationship to what they do at night or on weekends will provide them with a better conceptualization of time.

GA1335

Family Outings—Talk to children about activities that families do together. Write down the children's favorites on an overhead transparency or on the chalkboard. Once the data has been collected, prepare a bar graph which depicts the results of the classroom survey. Talk to children about graphs as being a form of communication which can be "read." If possible, make a similar survey in a classroom of older children and compare the results.

Activity	Numbers of Children							
	5		10	15	20	25	30	
Going on picnics								
Going to the movies								
Going to church								
Going to the park								
Going skating								
Going fishing								
Watching television								
Visiting grandparents								

The Classroom Family—Talk to children about the social relationships which occur because they are all together in one classroom. Help them understand that it is necessary to establish rules and that children need to be considerate of one another's feelings in order to work and play together effectively throughout the year.

Books for the Family Relationship Center:

Brown, Laurene Kransy, and Mark Brown. *Dinosaurs Divorce: A Guide for Changing Families.* New York: The Atlantic Monthly Press, 1986.

Carey, Valerie Scho. *Harriet and William and the Terrible Creature.* New York: Dutton, 1990.

Chorao, Kay. *George Told Kate.* New York: Dutton, 1990.

Christiansen, C.B. *My Mother's House, My Father's House.* New York: Puffin, 1990.

Cleary, Beverly. *Ramona the Pest.* New York: William Morrow & Company, 1982.

DuQuette, Keith. *A Ripping Day for a Picnic.* New York: Viking, 1990.

Gauch, Patricia Lee. *Christina Katerina & the Box.* New York: Coward-McCann & Geoghegan, Inc., 1971.

Hill, Elizabeth Shaw. *Evan's Corner.* New York: Viking, 1990.

Kandoian, Ellen. *Maybe She Forgot.* New York: Cobblehill, 1990.

Kingman, Lee. *Catch the Baby!* New York: Viking, 1990.

Levine, Abby. *What Did Mommy Do Before You?* New York: Puffin, 1990.

Lobel, Arnold. *Frog and Toad Are Friends.* New York: Harper and Row, 1986.

Munsch, Robert. *I Love You Forever.* New York: Fire Fly Books, 1989.

Olson, Arielle North. *Hurry Home, Grandma.* New York: Dutton, 1990.

Peterson, Jeanne Whitehouse. *I Have a Sister. My Sister Is Deaf.* New York: Harper and Row, 1977.

Rippon, Penelope. *My Day.* New York: Viking, 1990.

Rogers, Fred. *Making Friends.* New York: G.P. Putnam's Sons, 1987.

Rosenberg, Maxine. *Being Adopted.* New York: Lothrop, Lee & Shepard Books, 1984.

Sage, Chris. *Happy Baby.* New York: Dial, 1990.

_____ . *Sleepy Baby.* New York: Dial, 1990.

Sobol, Harriet Langsam. *My Brother Steven Is Retarded.* New York: Macmillan Publishing Company, 1977.

_____ . *We Don't Look Like Our Mom and Dad.* New York: Coward-McCann Company, 1984.

Stein, Sara Bonnett. *The Adopted One.* New York: Walker & Company, 1979.

Steptoe, Joseph. *Stevie.* New York: Harper and Row, 1986.

Turner, Gwenda. *Once upon a Time.* New York: Viking, 1990.

Wood, Audrey. *The Napping House.* New York: Harcourt Brace Jovanovich, 1989.

GA1335

School Center

Going to school is such a big step! It's a rite of passage that presents competent versus incompetent feelings within children and mixed feelings of pride and concern for their parents. Children are leaving home and encountering the world on their own for the the first time. Are they ready for it? Will they be successful?

The School Center presents an opportunity for children to resolve conflicts they are having about school in a play setting. They learn the special skills which older siblings and friends already know by learning to follow directions, learning to work together with others, and practicing skills needed for schoolwork. All these experiences are invaluable to children so that they can feel more confident in the larger group setting.

The purposes of the School Center are as follows:

To assist children in developing healthy attitudes about school and the learning they do in school

To serve as a transition area for children who have difficulties in large groups

To emphasize the responsibilities that each has in the school setting

To give children the understanding that groups of people must work together in order to have a happy relationship in school

To reinforce specific skills which relate to school success

To help children overcome initial fears they have about going to school

Here's what you need to prepare the School Center.

Small table and chair, two or three desks, shelves for books

Chalkboard and chalk

Suitable props which help the area resemble a school (a flag, books, wastebasket, rug for circle area, a plant or flowers for the "teacher's" desk, a small bell, rulers, yardstick, meterstick, etc.)

Pencils, paper of all types, crayons, scissors, paste or glue, erasers

Charts of paper or poster board

Articles of clothing which will enhance role play

Corkboard for messages (this could become a permanent part of the classroom when the School Center is disassembled)

Books—commercial, teacher-made, and child-made

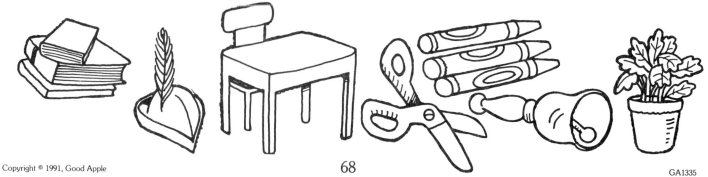

GA1335

A typical floor plan for the School Center might look like the following:

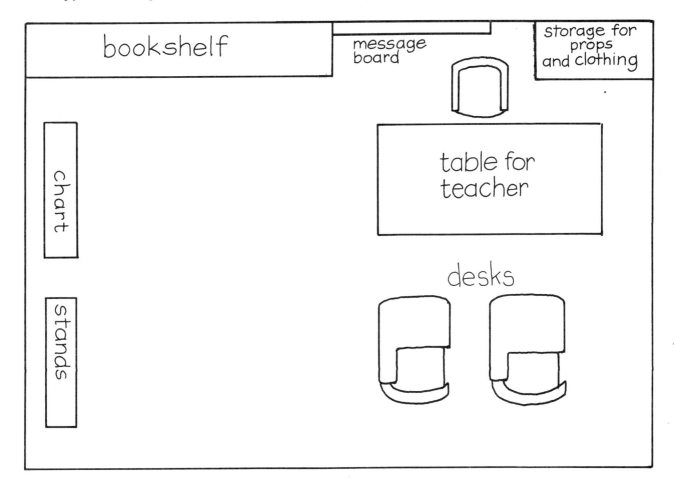

Here are some ideas to try to enhance language learning.

Let's Play School—A section of the learning center should be reserved for children to simply play school. A desk, small chalkboard, books, a jacket of any type and art supplies can add realism to the area. One child can put on the glasses and jacket and pretend to be the teacher while the other child (or perhaps two children) can be the students. After a period of time (perhaps a simple timer should be used), the children can rotate their roles. It will be interesting to observe the mannerisms of the children in this setting, as many times insight into one's own teaching style is revealed.

Learning to Work Together—One of the major functions of our educational system is to help individuals learn to work together. For the young learner, this can be a long and difficult undertaking. The purpose of these center activities is to give children (in groups of two or three) tasks that will require them to work together.

Set up two bowls on a table. One should be filled with sand or water. With two or three spoons (depending on the number of children involved), one child should take a spoon, transfer the sand from the full bowl to the second child's spoon who will then put the sand in the empty bowl. When the other bowl is filled, the task is ended. While very simplistic in nature, the children work together to complete a task.

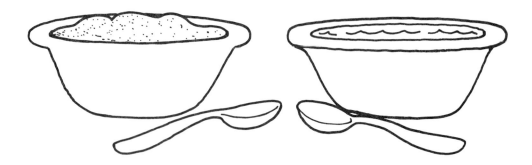

Give a description of a picture to color or paint to two or three children. The description should include several items. An example would be for the children to paint a picture of a dog that is in the woods with a rainbow and clouds overhead. Should the children be nonreaders, the caregiver could use a cassette recorder to give the directions. Children must then paint simultaneously on the same piece of paper to be able to complete the task. Each member of the team must decide which features he or she is responsible for. When difficulties arise, the teacher makes suggestions on how to share the responsibility, but she allows children to decide for themselves how the problem will be solved.

Another activity which requires the children to work together is to take a puzzle and divide the parts equally (one for you and one for me). Together, they must complete the puzzle with each child participating.

GA1335

The teacher should record a series of messages for the children to listen to. Each segment on the tape will give the children a message in two parts. One child will take the first part of the message; the other, the second. Both halves must be given for the message to make sense. For instance, a taped message could require one child to say, "If it doesn't rain today," and the other finish by saying, "Do you think we can go out and play?" The complexity of the message depends on the ability of the children involved. Second graders could work together to record the two halves of the message.

Following Directions—One area that poses difficulties for many children is learning to follow directions. This section of the learning center will provide opportunities for one child to give directions and another to follow them and then to reverse the roles. Basically, these activities are designed to promote listening skills.

Place five objects of different sizes and shapes on the table in the School Center along with sequence cards which show pictures of the objects in varying orders. One of the two children will wear a blindfold (which the teacher may need to place on the child's eyes) while the other will select a card that shows the objects in a particular order. The child holding the card gives oral directions for placing the objects in the order found on the card. The blindfolded child uses his sense of touch to put the objects in the correct order. After each sequence is complete, the roles are reversed.

Another activity for following directions involves listening to recordings of songs that require children to perform certain tasks or playing Simon Says with no losers. These songs and games may be more appropriate for the class as a whole or during times where additional noise is appropriate.

Prepare a set of simple task cards which requires children to bend and touch their toes, close one eye, hop on one foot, skip around the table, tie a shoe, raise one hand and one foot, walk like a duck, etc. Each of these requires developmentally appropriate movement and are accomplished by following directions. Children can work in pairs or threes with one child "reading" the pictures from the task card and the other child(ren) performing the actions.

71

GA1335

Classroom Jobs—Set up a three-dimensional model of the classroom on the floor or on a small table in the School Center. Using poster board for the base, furniture, fixtures and walls, the children will be looking down on a model of their classroom without a roof. While accuracy is not paramount, it is important children know what the symbols represent (tables, chairs, desks, trash can, etc.). Each small group of children should be required to organize the room (to the best of their abilities) to look like the real one once they have completed their task cards. The major purpose of this activity is to assist the children in understanding that the classroom's appearance is everyone's responsibility or job.

One child is to read or follow the pictorial directions on the task card and set the scene as described by the card. The other child is to correct the situation and state verbally why. Pairs of children should make a mutual decision about when they will change roles.

Card 1—It is the end of the school day and there is trash all over the floor.

Card 2—Children have been running in the classroom and three tables are turned over.

Card 3—The children enter the school one morning and all of the furniture has been moved around.

Card 4—The children are getting ready for lunch and discover that they have books everywhere.

Card 5—The fire marshall has visited the classroom and says the children could not get out of the room safely.

Card 6—A new child is coming to school and is in your room. Where should the new student sit? Whose table would be the best one to help a new person?

Card 7—It is the end of the day and there is writing on all of the chalkboards. What should be done?

Other cards and situations can be added at the teacher's discretion. Each team should be encouraged to discuss their actions and decisions. Time should also be allotted for the children to have free play with this model as many basic mapping skills are also being taught.

GA1335

Teacher for the Day—Select a child who will be teacher for the day. When the School Center is open, this individual will be the "teacher" in role playing situations, but special errands and privileges (being line leader, for example) can be given to the selected teacher. Give every child in the classroom an opportunity to be "teacher," but also accept the child's right to refuse the position.

Being Nice to Others—The teacher should develop a series of situational cards which present certain classroom situations for the students to resolve. If the children are nonreaders, a cassette recorder or pictures may be used. The goal is for the children to verbalize solutions to the situations presented. Since the children will be working in groups of two or three, the teacher should encourage them to develop their own solutions and provide a rationale for their decisions. Suggested situations are

> a student drops a pencil on the floor and no one notices
>
> someone accidentally pushes a child down
>
> the teacher is talking and you want to ask a question
>
> two of your friends are howling like dogs during quiet time and you want to join in
>
> a student loses money on the playground
>
> a student is riding a toy on the playground for a long time while others wait their turns
>
> a student is shoving in line

Each of these situations (as well as countless others) will arise throughout the school year. Assisting children in recognizing trouble situations and verbalizing possible solutions and considering the feelings of others is a step toward greater understanding of one another.

Books for the School Center:

Ahlberg, Allan, and Janet Ahlberg. *Starting School.* New York: Puffin, 1990.

Hennessy, B.G. *School Days.* New York: Viking, 1990.

Rockwell, Harlow. *My Nursery School.* New York: Greenwillow Books, 1976.

Van Leeuwen, Jean. *Oliver Pig at School.* New York: Dial, 1990.

Neighborhood Center

Children's first experiences outside their homes are usually in their neighborhood. They come to school knowing about the families that live near them and where the business establishments are which they frequent on a regular basis. Except for large cities where children often do not know their neighbors, children enter school with friends from their neighborhoods which they have known for several years.

Becoming better acquainted with one's neighborhood is pleasurable. Children have working knowledge of their neighborhoods because they have experiences in them. What this center does with the study of neighborhoods is to assist children in clarifying misconceptions they have about neighborhoods and to broaden their understanding of what goes on in their worlds.

The purposes of the Neighborhood Center are as follows:

To help children understand the concept of neighborhood and neighbors

To provide opportunities for children to tell what they know about their neighborhoods

To encourage interaction among children who are probably neighbors because they go to the same school or center

To help children become more aware of the adult roles which they can observe in their environment

To help children develop an understanding that there is a world broader than their homes and they are members of this world

To associate what children know about neighborhoods with the print that is all around them

Here's what you need to prepare the Neighborhood Center.

Pictures of business establishments and adults performing their jobs to place on a bulletin board

Table suitable for placing several boxes of varying sizes which will serve as businesses, homes, public buildings, and other representations of neighborhood living

Small dolls for symbolic play (paper dolls could substitute)

Articles of clothing which would allow children to role-play fire fighters, police officers, mail carriers, doctors, nurses, businessmen and women, plumbers, carpenters, etc.

Traffic signs placed around the room for role play

Optional, but useful, materials: bring in two or three large refrigerator or freezer boxes for children to paint and use as business establishments and public vehicles

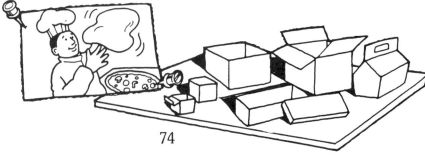

GA1335

A typical floor plan for the Neighborhood Center might look like the following:

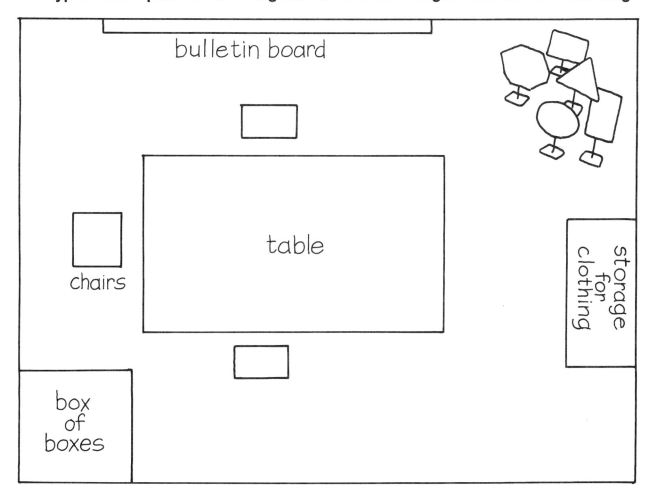

Here are some ideas to try to enhance language learning.

A Neighbor Is Someone Who Lives Next Door—Talk to children about who neighbors are. Ask them to tell who their neighbor is in the classroom. Invite them to talk about their neighbors at home. If children are unsure about who their neighbors are, request that they ask their parents about their neighbors, and when they are ready to report, allow them to do so. Give them an opportunity to describe their neighborhoods as well. Ask children to draw pictures of their neighbors and collect these into a booklet. If children live close to one another, group their pictures together in the booklet so that a sense of neighborhood can be developed by looking at the booklet.

A Neighborhood Is Where People Live—To assist the children in understanding that any dwelling can be a home, the caregiver will provide butcher paper with the title "A Neighborhood Is a Place Where People Live." Each small group of children (suggest working in teams of three) will be given a picture of a type of dwelling (country homes, city homes, trailers, apartments, big homes, little homes, town houses, etc.). Once the small group receives their card, they can work on their section of the mural any time they are permitted. Their goal is to find pictures in magazines, newspapers, real estate advertisements and brochures from the Chamber of Commerce to cut and paste on their section. Should pictures be hard to find, the children can use or paint additional dwellings.

After the children complete their mural, it should be hung on a wall in the classroom for display purposes. It also provides an opportunity for the caregiver and children to talk about the many dwellings where people live. If there are pictures available of the children in the class, each can be placed in the section of the mural that represents the type of dwelling where each child lives. It is important that pride be associated with where one lives.

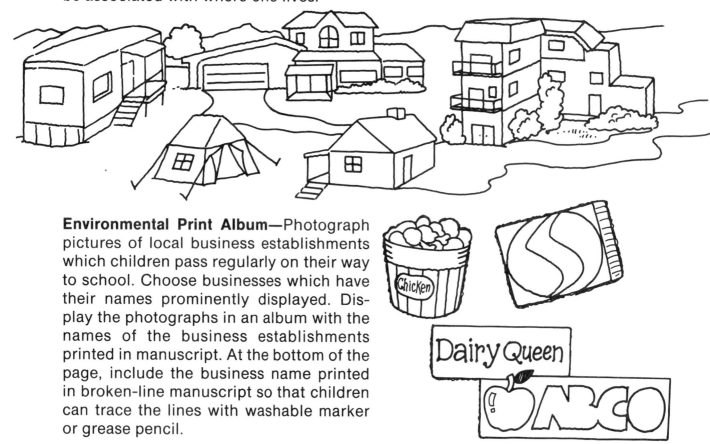

Environmental Print Album—Photograph pictures of local business establishments which children pass regularly on their way to school. Choose businesses which have their names prominently displayed. Display the photographs in an album with the names of the business establishments printed in manuscript. At the bottom of the page, include the business name printed in broken-line manuscript so that children can trace the lines with washable marker or grease pencil.

Community Spirit—Bring in brochures, advertising flyers, business cards, stationery from local businesses, and other paraphernalia to display on a bulletin board in the Neighborhood Center for children to look at and "read." Ask them to bring in other items to add to the board. If possible, plan a field trip to a community fair or athletic event so that children can gain a better perspective of the community in action.

GA1335

A Neighborhood Is Where People Work—Provide grocery sacks (one for each child), paints or crayons, scissors and glue. If at all possible, pictures, advertisements, product sacks and equipment should be placed on a table in this section of the learning center to represent the different jobs that can be found in the neighborhood.

The caregiver may want to talk about the different materials found in this section of the center with the entire class to acquaint them with the many jobs that are required in a neighborhood. In addition to the police, fire fighters and postal workers, the teacher should include custodians, city workers, those who pick up trash, cooks, clerks, ministers, white collar professionals, and any other individuals who work in the neighborhood.

Each child will take a paper sack and decorate it to look like something the worker would wear. Pictures found in books, magazines and newspapers can provide children with ideas. The paper sacks can be colored or painted and trimmed with construction paper. Once the projects have been completed, the children can slip on their worker's clothes and display to other groups. Encourage children to tell other children one thing their worker does in the neighborhood.

At Circle Time, ask children to tell what jobs their parents hold in the community. Making a chart of the various jobs represented in the class will provide another print experience.

A Neighborhood Has Streets and Buildings—This section of the learning center will require boxes of all types (from matchboxes to shoe boxes to oatmeal containers), crayons, paints, magic markers and a piece of plywood at least four feet (1.22 m) square. With these aids, the caregiver will help the children create their own neighborhood. Should the school be located in the neighborhood where children live, it can serve as a focal point of the project. Should the school be in a more isolated location, the caregiver can select a landmark or building that is familiar to most of the children.

With this previous information in mind, the teacher should take a box and place it in a central location where the landmark or school can be found. Then she should take a magic marker and start drawing the streets around the central location. If possible, this step should be completed with all the children watching so she can explain to them which procedures should be undertaken. Once completed, the plywood should now look like the neighborhood without any buildings.

Following this, the caregiver should help the children in naming the buildings in their neighborhood and write those names in their approximate location on the plywood. Should the children not be able to read the names, pictures or symbols may be used. What this step accomplishes is to provide the children with the location of the buildings they will be creating individually or in small groups.

Depending on the number of buildings to be included, each small group can select (or be assigned) a building they are responsible for making. Then they can color or paint or decorate the building with construction paper to look like the structure they are responsible for. Once completed, they can place the building on the location designated by the name or picture or symbol. When all of the small groups complete their assignments, the neighborhood is formed.

The last phase of this project is to take the matchboxes to make cars, buses and trucks to place on the streets of their neighborhood. Depending on the developmental levels of the children, signs, trees and people can be added as well. Barbie and Ken type dolls, paper dolls, or handmade puppets from the Puppet Center would yield wonderful symbolic play.

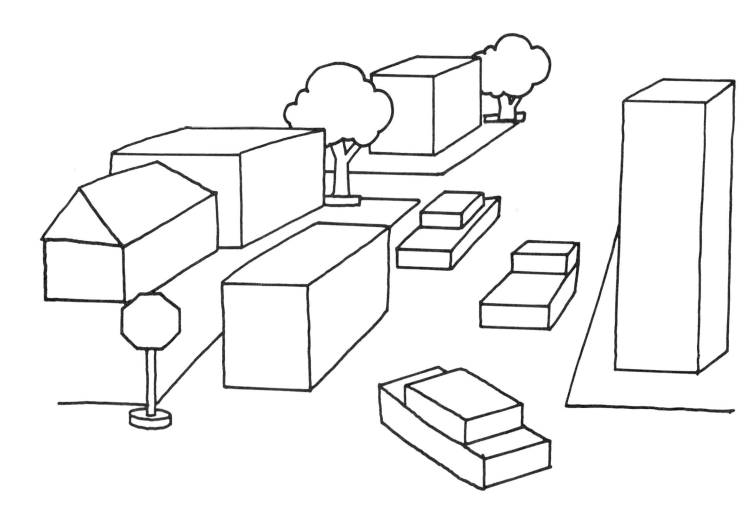

A Neighborhood Is for People to Be Proud Of—Because of the nature of this center, the caregiver may want to invite the parents or guardians to visit the school to view the projects their children have developed. Allow children to wear their uniforms and tell the group at least one thing the workers in the neighborhoods do. Also, their mural will allow the children to share with their loved ones the places people in their neighborhoods live and then show what their neighborhoods look like.

Lending a Helping Hand—Develop a discussion with children about what being a good neighbor means. Use current events in the community to emphasize how citizens have helped others in a time of crisis or emergency. Brainstorm with children specific ways that children could be good neighbors in their neighborhoods and write these on a chart.

Assist children in selecting a project they can do to show that they are good neighbors. Options might be:

bringing in food for needy families

adopting an animal at the local zoo

collecting pet supplies for the local animal shelter

organizing a cleanup campaign in the neighborhood or playground

planning a garage sale at the school or center

collecting aluminum cans to earn money for their school

Once the project is selected, talk to the children about the need to write letters to the principal, teachers in the school, and their parents to elicit their support for the project. Include a letter to the editor of the local newspaper about the class project. While carrying out the plans which the class has made, be sure to record information about what is being done and when. A record of expenditures may be in order as well. Special flyers could be necessary with some projects for distribution in the neighborhood.

When the project is over, follow-up thank-you letters are important and emphasize another need for writing.

Books for the Neighborhood Center:

All Around the Neighborhood. Bank Street College of Education Editors. New York: Barron, 1985.

Brown, Margaret W. *Home for Bunny.* New York: A Golden Book, 1983.

Cooke, Tom. *I Want a Hat Like That.* New York: A Sesame Street/Golden Book, 1987.

Ventura, Piero. *Piero Ventura's Book of Cities.* New York: Random House, 1975.

Wallner, John. *City Mouse, Country Mouse and Two More Tales from Aesop.* New York: Scholastic, Inc., 1987.

Transportation Center

Wheels hold an attraction for humans and have since the time of their discovery. Among the first toys children receive are wagons, scooters, tricycles and all manner of vehicles. Pedaling faster than the wind, rolling joyfully along the sidewalk, breezing around the playground with as much speed as the child can muster—these are the delights of childhood.

No wonder humans have continued to build machines which will take them faster and further then they traveled yesterday. The Transportation Center provides for the wanderlust in the soul!

The purposes of the Transportation Center are as follows:

To help children learn about the variety of transportation modes

To give children information about the economic, business and pleasure reasons transportation exists

To let children verbalize what they already know about transportation

To allow children the experience of moving on transportation-type equipment

To help children understand the needs for safety when traveling in moving vehicles

To remind children about traffic safety and what their responsibilities are when they are on the street

To provide for verbal and written interactions among children about what they are learning

Here's what you need to prepare a Transportation Center.

Wheeled toys (tricycles, wagons, scooters, bicycles for older children, etc.)

Pictures of transportation vehicles

Traffic signs (Commercial varieties are available, but they can be teacher-made.)

Cardboard boxes of various sizes to make representations of cars, trucks, trains, boats, etc.

Miniature cars, trucks, trains, boats, airplanes, etc.

A typical floor plan for the Transportation Center might look like the following:

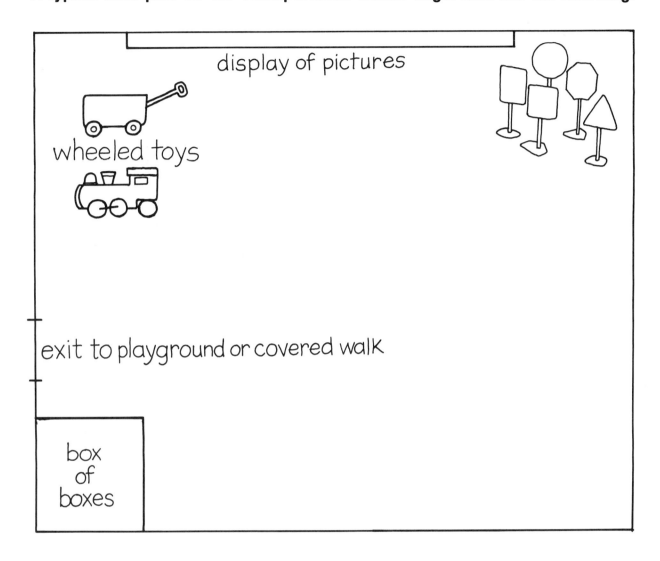

Think Big—Understand the child's need for realism in play activity. Bring real vehicles to school, if possible. Teachers of young children have been known to park an eighteen wheeler on the kindergarten playground for about two weeks so that children can climb, explore, play, and find out as much as possible about the truck. Make a rowboat a part of the permanent equipment on the playground. Ask the school to let your class come to the bus barn and look under the hood and wheel bases of one of the buses. Invite the local fire chief to bring a fire truck to the school campus. Plan for every child to have a trip on the truck and sound the siren if he chooses. If train travel is possible, plan a trip to a nearby town. Visit an airport (even small ones are interesting to learn about).

Put a few old tires on the playground so that children can roll them. Find a tub for "boat play." Bring a horse or pony to school one afternoon so that children can have a ride. Second graders are capable of trying roller skates and stilts. Transportation is an enjoyable study!

 GA1335

The Ways We Travel on Land and the Things We Move—This section of the center will focus on the ways people travel on land and the different things moved from one place to another. In addition to several picture books, the caregiver will need newspapers, magazines, brochures from car and truck dealerships and old catalogs. After placing the previously mentioned materials on a table, the children will be instructed to take a piece of butcher paper and divide it in two columns. The first column is for the children to identify the types of transportation that are used for people to move from one place to another (cars, buses, bicycles, taxis, etc.) The second is for children to identify other forms of land transportation and the things that are moved (log trucks, automobile carriers, moving vans, tank trucks, dump trucks, etc.).

Using newspapers, catalogs, brochures and magazines, small groups of children (in twos or threes) will identify as many forms of transportation that move people as they can. The pictures will be glued on the appropriate column. Once the first column is completed, children should search for types of land transportation that move other things. Should they think of products that are moved and not be able to locate a picture, they can draw or paint a representation. Encourage the children to share their information with other children and compare efforts. If children are able to write, they may wish to label the types of transportation identified or create a story about a type of transportation.

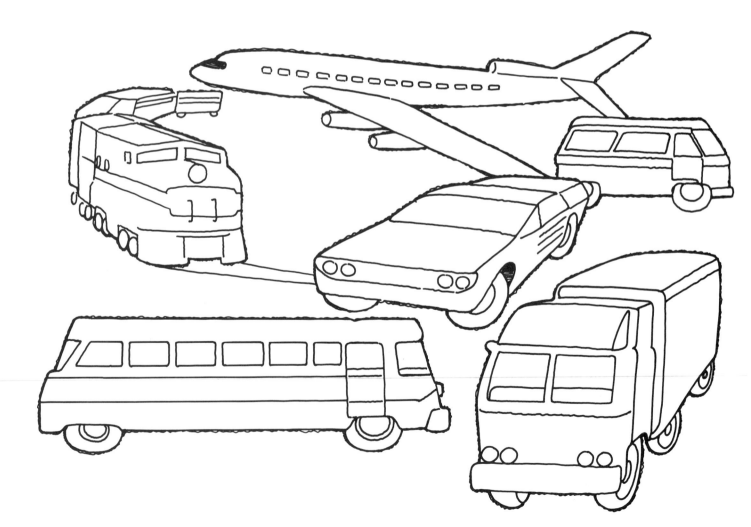

The Ways We Travel in the Air—Even though we are an extremely mobile society, there are many children who have never seen or been on an airplane. As a result, the caregiver will want to make sure she has as many support materials as possible for this section of the learning center. To complete this portion of the center, the teacher will need two coat hangers for each small group of children, poster board cut in pieces approximately four inches (10.16 cm) square, yarn, scissors, hole punch and glue. For recess or free time, the teacher may want to have several types of paper airplanes available for the children to learn more about the basic principles of flight.

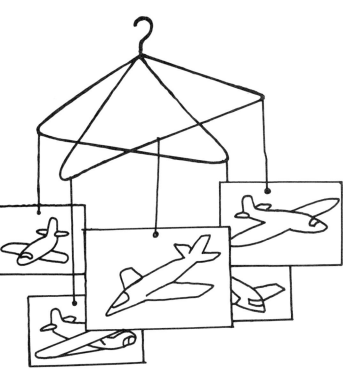

With brochures and other information provided by travel agencies, airplane periodicals and airline companies, the small groups of children can cut pictures of different types of airplanes and paste them on each side of the small paper squares. A hole should be made in the top portion of each of the squares and yarn attached. Once that is completed, the two coat hangers should be crisscrossed to form the foundation of a mobile that will hold five cards displaying ten different airplanes. Encourage each group of children to share their mobiles and any information they may have learned about the planes. Once the projects are completed, the caregiver can hang the mobiles from the ceiling to display the children's work in a prominent manner.

As an alternative to the pictures being glued on the poster board, the caregiver can use cardboard or poster board to make patterns of different types of airplanes for the children to trace, cut and then hang on the mobile.

GA1335

For Teacher Use Only

Use the following patterns for children to trace and cut out for mobiles. Cutting on lines is an excellent prewriting experience for nonwriters and gives writers needed practice in eye-hand coordination.

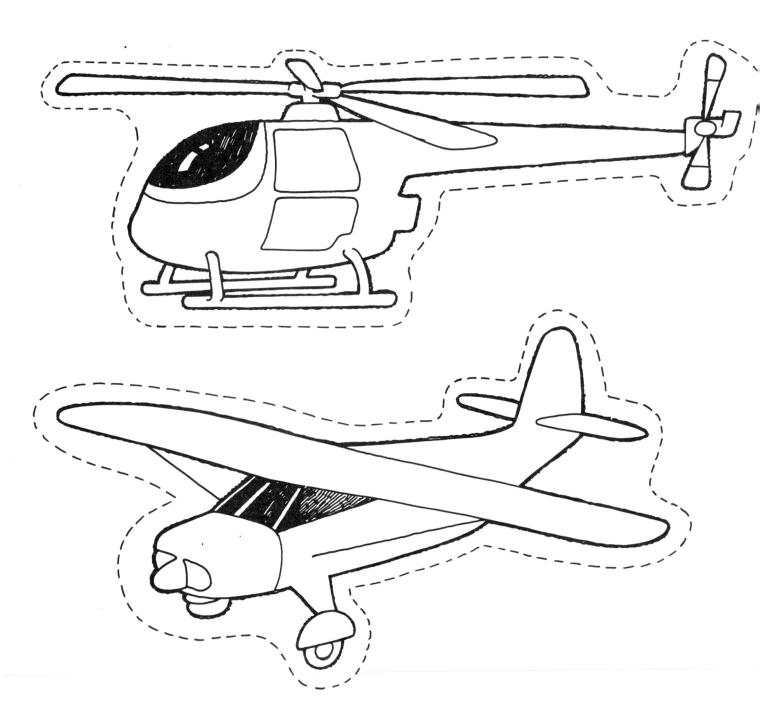

84

GA1335

85

GA1335

The Ways We Travel by Train—Add several shoe boxes of different sizes, small round containers (like empty Pringles cans), crayons or paints, small boxes (empty matchboxes), construction paper of different colors and patterns for wheels, smoke-stacks, animals and logs to the Transportation Center.

Encourage the children to construct their own trains and rail cars out of the materials mentioned above. Depending on the time and interest levels, each group can make their own train with two or three cars or a particular type of car for a class train. They can paint their round box or container and then decorate their particular car to look like the ones they have seen in the books. To do this, they can add the wheels, products, animals, cars or fuel (possibly a coal bin). If the locomotive is an older type, they can add a smokestack and front grill. Some of the cars for the groups to construct can include those that move people, fuel, animals, pipes, cars and other products the children may have encountered in their books.

Once their project has been allowed to dry, they can connect the class or group train and share their results with the other children. If the caregiver desires, she can read a story about a train (like the *Pony Engine*) and the children can take turns acting out the story while the story is being read.

An alternative would be for the children to make up their own story and share with other groups. All in all, this segment of the center is an excellent way to provide a culminating activity for the many things that can be learned about trains and the ways they help us transport people and things from one place to another.

Ships, Ahoy—To set up this area of the center, the teacher will need easels, paper for paintings, colors, small bits of paper for decorations, scissors, glue and old boating magazines. The first task the small groups or individuals will need to complete is to select a type of boat that has been identified (fishing boats, tugboats, ocean liners, tankers, battleships, etc.) in one of the old magazines.

Next, they will paint a picture of the boat on the provided paper and allow it to dry. Then the children are to paint a piece of paper blue (or take a piece of blue construction paper) and cut it up in small pieces. After completing this task, they are to glue the pieces of paper on the painting to give the appearance of water. Other colors of paint can be used and the procedure repeated for the sun, smoke, products, moon and/or stars.

GA1335

After they have finished their paintings, the children are to make up a short story that tells about their boat and how it is helpful to others. If the children are writers, they can write the story and share with the class or other small groups. If they are younger, they can dictate their story to the teacher for her to share with the others or for each group to share among themselves.

Throughout the period of time the children are learning about transportation, they should be encouraged to bring in models, pictures, books, artifacts or anything else that can be displayed in the center and shared with the other children. Should one of the children have a parent or guardian who has worked or currently works with boats, he/she could be asked to come to the class and share his/her expertise.

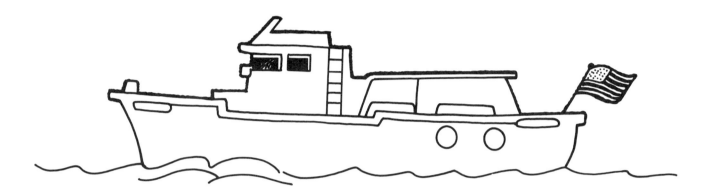

Books for the Transportation Center:

Burton, Virginia Lee. *Mike Mulligan and His Steam Shovel.* Boston: Houghton Mifflin Company, 1987.

Cole, Joanna. *Cars and How They Go.* New York: Crowell Company, 1983.

Crews, Donald. *Flying.* New York: Greenwillow Books, 1986.

Ford, Frances M. (adapted by Doris Garn). *The Pony Engine.* Los Angeles: Wonder Books, 1987.

Magee, Doug, and Robert Newman. *All Aboard ABC.* New York: Cobblehill, 1990.

Munro, Roxie. *Blimps.* New York: E.P. Dutton, 1989.

Piper, Watty. *The Little Engine That Could.* New York: Putnam, 1988.

Rockwell, Anne. *Planes.* New York: E.P. Dutton, 1985.

_____ . *Things That Go.* New York: E.P. Dutton, 1986.

Schceier, Joshua. *Luigi's All-Night Parking Lot.* New York: Dutton, 1990.

Seymour, Peter. *Fire Fighter.* New York: Lodestar, 1990.

Smith, Jesse. *Going Places.* New York: A Sesame Street/Golden Press Book, 1988.

Zelinsky, Paul O., III. *The Wheels on the Bus.* New York: Dutton, 1990.

Personal Health and Safety Center

Many of the attitudes children form about keeping care of their bodies are set in the early years. Having a unit of study about health and safety is important because it reinforces what is being taught at home for some children and for others the information may only be learned at school. Determining what is age appropriate for children to understand is the key ingredient in developing healthy attitudes toward health and safety.

The teacher's attitude about health and safety is as essential to this study as the knowledge that is being presented. If teachers can show children how they take care of themselves and emphasize the need for daily care, even when this study is completed, then children will continue to develop new understandings of health and safety as it relates to their lives. The long-term benefit is healthier children.

The purposes of the Personal Health and Safety Center are as follows:

To emphasize the need for daily routines in building healthy bodies

To help children understand basic rules which will prevent classroom, playground, and home accidents

To help children understand that health routines and safety practices are a lifetime endeavor

To give children knowledge which can be shared in their homes to improve their quality of life

To provide opportunities for children to talk and write about health and safety in their daily lives

Here's what you need to prepare a Personal Health and Safety Center.

Small table and chairs placed near a sink, if possible

Bulletin board (for displaying pictures which relate to health and safety)

Artifacts which relate to healthy living (toothpaste, dental floss, soap, deodorant, washcloths and towels, Q-tips, pillow and blanket, etc.)

Pictures or posters of the food groups (usually introduced to children after age five)

Medical items could include bandages, arm splints, crutches, a wheelchair, empty and clean containers of over-the-counter medications, gauze, prescription pads, cotton balls, or other items which children would possibly see in a doctor's office

Articles of clothing which could represent members of the medical profession (white jacket or uniform, surgical gown, stethoscope, etc.)

GA1335

A typical floor plan for the Personal Health and Safety Center might look like the following:

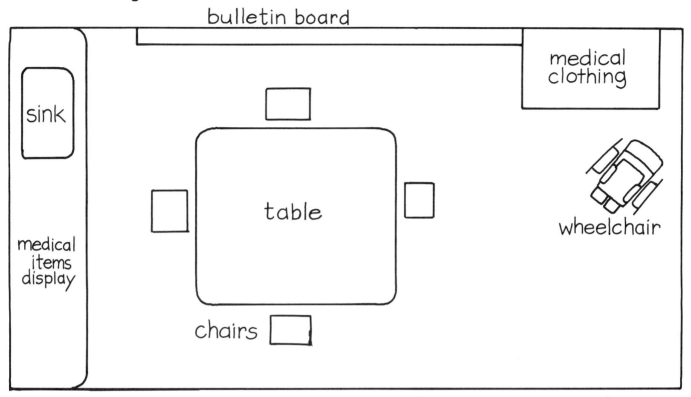

Here are some ideas to try to enhance language development.

Dental Health—Contact a local dentist who works with children to come into the classroom for a presentation. Inviting dentists to visit will establish the best knowledge base for the children because of the concrete examples they will bring to the classroom. Further, most dentists will give each child in the class a toothbrush, dental floss and a small tube of toothpaste. For some children this may be their first experience with dental hygiene, and reinforcing the knowledge they learn from the dentist is critical.

GA1335

If the classroom has its own sink, this portion of the learning center can be created around it. Should the classroom not have its own sink, the caregiver should have a pretend one set up on a rectangular table. Also needed will be a mirror and small signs or pictures that display the five steps to better smiles.

The first step is to have clean hands.

The second is to rinse the toothbrush prior to using.

The third is to put a small amount of toothpaste on the brush.

The fourth is to moisten the toothpaste and brush up and down and all around.

The fifth step is to rinse and dry the mouth.

If at all possible, the children should be allowed to brush their teeth after lunch. Even with the time demands, it is a habit worth developing. While the dentist will encourage flossing, it is not practical to do so at school, but the teacher can stress the need to do so at home.

As a follow-up activity, the children in small groups can write and illustrate stories about what they have learned about dental health and have the caregiver deliver the stories to the dentist as a thank-you for coming to the classroom. Should the children be nonwriters, they can use picture writing which illustrates an individual using good dental health practices.

GA1335

What Should We Do?—Invite the school nurse or an area doctor or nurse to come to the classroom to discuss some of the basic knowledge children should know about health. The teacher should brainstorm with the students the types of questions they would like to ask of a health specialist. Write down the children's questions so that they can be remembered. If children should need prompts, try some of these.

1. What should I do if I scrape my arm or leg? How do I put on a bandage or wrap?
2. What should I do if I fall really hard and hurt really bad (broken bones, concussion, etc.)?
3. What if there is blood when I get hurt? What if my nose just starts to bleed for no reason?
4. What should I do if I am stung by a wasp?
5. What should I do if I get really hot or cold?
6. What should I do if I get burned?
7. What should I do if I choke on my food?
8. What should I do if any of these things happen to a friend?
9. Is it okay for me to take medicine on my own or give some to my friends?
10. Why do I have to get shots?
11. Is it really important for me to be clean?
12. Do kids need to exercise?

Provide the doctor or nurse with a set of the children's questions prior to their visit.

What Should You Do?—On the table in the learning center, there should be bandages, an empty alcohol bottle, gauze for cleaning, an ice pack, a phone, a prescription pad, and other common items the doctor or nurse talked about. There should also be several What Should You Do? cards that allow small groups of children to role-play their actions in an injury or medical situation and the types of things they would share with a doctor or nurse (should they be suffering the injury or be describing the injury). The following represent several role-play ideas. Whenever possible, pictures and words should be incorporated.

If you scrape your arm and leg?	If your friend falls and hurts his head?
If you hurt yourself and you are bleeding?	If your friend's nose starts to bleed?

GA1335

If everyone is getting the measles and you haven't had them?	If your friend is eating and starts to choke?
If you feel bad and a friend offers you some of his medicine?	If there is a medical emergency and you need to call for help?
If someone needs you to clean a scrape and you have dirty hands?	If you get too hot playing?
If your friends want to lie around and watch television or play video games all of the time?	If you walk outdoors and it's cold?

Basically, each situation simply reviews what the health representative talked about. Working in groups of two or three allows the children to play different roles and discuss different solutions. The teacher needs to be observant of the children's actions during this activity so that she can intervene if children are making unwise decisions.

Personal Health by Eating—In this area of the learning center, the caregiver needs all types of food boxes (junk food included), soft drink cans and bottles (non-breakable), an empty jar of peanut butter and pictures of food laminated and mounted on poster board.

Small groups of children should be allowed to plan meals through free play and also directed through the following task cards (or the questions may be written on a chart):

What Should I Eat. . .

When I want to eat a snack?

When I need a quick, healthy breakfast?

When I am told to eat protein?

When I am told to eat vegetables?

When I need a quick, healthy lunch?

When I am hungry for dinner?

When I need to take my lunch to school?

To help build strong bones and teeth?

Small groups of children can use the boxes and pictures to plan their meals while also answering the task cards. Children can learn that nutritionists are now recognizing the role of fats and sweets in the diet and that the concept of a *fifth food group* is gaining popularity.

By acknowledging that the fifth food group exists, it's easier to learn how to control the fats and sweets by teaching children the negative impact they make if they are consumed in large quantities.

This activity is best introduced to children five and older. If children are non-readers, an aid or a parent volunteer can assist in the center by reading the specific questions children need to address in their role playing.

GA1335

Invite a Police Officer to School—Ask an officer to school and request that he or she address safety in a car, safety to and from school, bicycle safety and safety from those who may want to harm a child. If possible, the officer should also bring a police car to show to the children, giving them rides in it and opportunities to sound the siren. Since so much of what is learned here relates to a child's ability to act appropriately in a variety of situations, role playing will be encouraged extensively while the Personal Health and Safety Center is in the classroom.

Signs to Remember—After the officer has presented safety materials, use the table in the learning center to allow children to review what they have learned about important traffic signs. To accomplish this, the caregiver can display the sheet of traffic signs provided by the police officer and poster board patterns for children to use in the construction of their own set of signs. Using tagboard, children can trace and cut out their own set of signs. Then they can label them, paint them with appropriate colors and attach them to tongue depressors for display.

At this point, the children (in small groups) can play a cassette recording of different traffic situations and hold up the sign they should be looking for or sign that is needed. The cassette tape should also contain a self-check procedure. The children should be instructed to turn the tape off and on at specified times.

Examples of the situations contained on the tape are

    What sign should there be to keep people from driving too fast?
    What sign should there be when you come to a school?
    What sign should there be when the road makes a big curve?
    What sign should there be when the other driver has the right-of-way?
    What sign should there be near a play area?
    What sign should there be near a fire station?
    What sign should there be to let you know there is a crossroad ahead?

Other types of signs can be included as appropriate for older children. It is important not to require too many signs beyond the basics for younger children.

Safety to and from School—The teacher should supply a poster board that shows a map representation of the school and the street leading to the school. For the purpose of this center, accuracy is not as important as showing different routes to school with different traffic and safety alternatives to consider. Also needed for this activity are plastic children figures to move from one area to another, matchbox cars and situation cards for extension activities.

Because the police officer talked about safety to and from school, the poster board school map should show a busy street, a street passing by old buildings, a crosswalk where it is difficult to see traffic coming and a street where there are no sidewalks. In groups of two or three, the children are to take alternate routes to school and let one child explain what safety measures to take. Then the responsibility of explaining another route is rotated to another child.

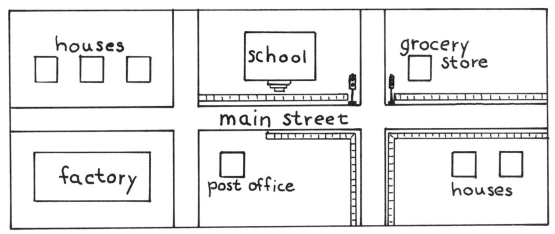

Following this activity, the children should be presented with several cards that describe traffic and safety situations for walkers and bicycle riders. Drawings or pictures can be used for the nonreader. The children are to describe what safety measures they would take if presented with the following situations:

Examples of situation cards are

Walking with small children	Walking on a street with no sidewalks
Walking when it is dark	Crossing streets with no traffic signs

Crossing streets with traffic lights

Riding a bicycle to school with no sidewalks

Riding a bicycle to school when it is getting dark

Crossing busy streets with traffic lights on a bicycle

Riding a bicycle to school when it is getting dark

Crossing streets with no lights on a bicycle

Car and Bicycle Safety Checks—The police officer who visits the classroom will provide the caregiver with packets of information for the children that have to do with bicycle and automobile safety. Since they are prepared for children, the pictures and dialogue should be easy for them to read, and if not, the pictures are descriptive enough to provide them with basic safety rules.

If at all possible, the teacher should bring a bicycle to class, a safety helmet and two or three types of safety belts for the automobile. She will then review the safety procedures for the bicycle and then show the children how they are to buckle up for safety. In some cases, the police officer will let the caregiver borrow a seat belt that can be easily attached to a chair.

After a large group display or the safety checks and procedures, the teacher can put the equipment in a section of the learning center for the children to practice with. A basic checklist can be developed on tagboard (for example, chain is tight, air in the tires, the handlebar is tight, the brakes work, a helmet is available, there are safety reflectors) for the children to use as a guide. Develop several situations so that they can verify their understanding of safety belt use through discussion or role play. These can be written on a chart or task cards or given to the children orally. Encourage children to develop their own situations.

Examples are as follows:

1. You are going for a ride with no safety belt.
2. A friend wants you to ride his bicycle.
3. Your mother puts a baby in the back seat of the car.
4. Your bicycle brakes do not work.
5. You are riding in a car with the doors not locked.
6. Your father leaves you in a car in the hot weather.

By listening carefully to the discussion, the caregiver can determine when clarifications need to be made. Allowing children to discuss all possible options helps children develop more flexible thinking skills.

Stranger Safety—Of all the materials that have been developed for children in recent years that deal with stranger safety, a crime dog is probably the best known. The materials developed are clear and easy for children to understand. Again, the caregiver should share these with the children and then provide the children opportunities to practice the rules in the learning center. Some of the situations for application are

1. A stranger offers you a ride.
2. You get lost.
3. A stranger offers you candy.
4. A stranger comes to your house.
5. A stranger offers you a toy.
6. A stranger offers to buy you ice cream.
7. A stranger tells you that your parents sent him or her.

Fire Safety—Using materials made available from the fire department, the same procedures should be applied as the other sections of the center. The rules should be reviewed in a large group and practiced in small groups. Some of the situations to check understanding are

1. You wake up at night and smell smoke.
2. You discover that you do not have smoke alarms.
3. One of your friends is playing with matches.
4. You discover a small fire near the stove.
5. You want to burn trash.

Personal Health Through Exercise—Extend what is being learned in the Personal Health and Safety Center by asking children to demonstrate the following activities on the playground. Alert parents that these activities will be occurring so that children can dress in casual clothing.

bounce a large ball (individually and to others)

hop in place on one foot

hop like a rabbit

jump in place

skip (for older fives)

run from one place to another (not racing)

clap or keep a simple rhythm (can be accompanied with "jam box" and simple songs)

GA1335

walking backwards

moving left and then right

walking like crabs, camels, elephants

moving like a snake (use a mat in the classroom for this activity)

rolling (use a mat in the classroom for this activity)

Of all of the centers found in this book, none is more important for your children. Therefore, if the suggestions do not exactly fit your class, alter them to accommodate their developmental levels. If they cannot read, make cassette tapes for them to use or read the material to them. Encourage them to think of situations where they can apply the rules that you may not think of. Extensions of this center can include gun safety, home safety, safety during play and many others. The needs of your children should dictate what should be included.

A practical way to culminate the entire study of health and safety would be for the children to make a mural to display the many safety ideas they have learned. Small groups can be responsible for one section of the learning center activities and share their thoughts with others. Once the mural is completed and displayed, the caregiver may want to review the contents from time to time to reinforce the importance of practicing safety procedures at all times. If children are writing, encouraging them to write stories about health and safety will extend the learning they are acquiring.

Books for the Personal Health and Safety Center:

Baher, Amy C. *Sometimes It's OK to Tell Secrets.* New York: Grosset and Dunlap, 1986.

_____ . *What Should You Do When . . . ?* New York: Grosset and Dunlap, 1986.

Communication and Sounds Center

The technological advances our culture has been witnessing within recent years are astounding, and as a consequence, children are growing up in an age that literally explodes with communication advances and sounds. They have been watching television since the day they were born, and their minds are bombarded with information on a daily basis. What children do with this information becomes the responsiblity of parents and teachers alike. Otherwise, what children have observed becomes another example of noise pollution.

Channeling the knowledge they are acquiring into appropriate learning means that they need to learn to talk and write about what they have seen on television. Learning about sounds and how they are made will also assist children in establishing rudimentary information about the communications industry. The Communication and Sounds Center should help them do both.

The purposes of the Communication and Sounds Center are as follows:

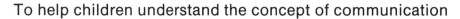

To help children understand the concept of communication

To provide children with opportunities to experiment with communication in a variety of forms

To develop vocabulary which accompanies the topic

To promote an understanding of the need for people everywhere to communicate with one another

To help children become better listeners in communication settings

To help children recognize that writing is also communication and how it relates to human speech

To allow children to gain confidence with the communication skills that they already possess

Here's what you need to prepare a Communication and Sounds Center.

Tables and chairs for display of communication items

Bulletin board to display pictures of communication types

Telephone (as realistic as possible) and telephone directory

Radio, cassette recorder, tapes, hearing aids (if available), megaphone, microphone, portable television, tin can telephones, funnel, noisemakers, walkie talkies, etc.

Manuscript chart and writing materials (paper and pencils)

A typical floor plan for the Communication and Sounds Center might look like the following:

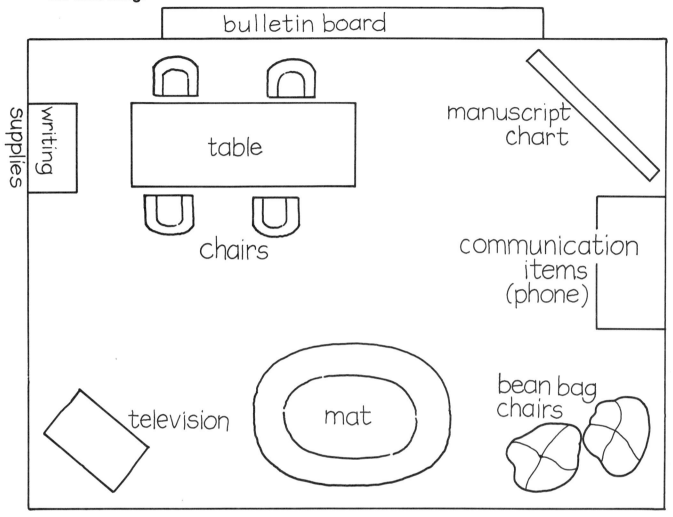

Here are some ideas to try to enhance language learning.

Communicating with Our Facial Expressions—One of the most common ways we communicate with others is through our facial expressions. To help children learn more about this form of communication, this section of the learning center will include pictures, cards describing an emotion, and the opportunity for children to paint or draw pictures displaying various emotions.

On a table in the learning center, the caregiver should have several laminated pictures of different facial expressions. In groups of two or three, the children are to select a picture and tell the others in the group what that facial expression is communicating to them. In some cases, there may be more than one answer.

For older children, words and facial expressions shown on cards can be included. Facial expressions can be shown well on paper plate puppets. Each child in the group is to select a card (or puppet) and attempt to communicate the expression to the other children in the small group. After the expression has been guessed, another child selects a card and the procedure is repeated. Some of the expressions to include are

anger   surprise   pain

confusion   fear   pleasure

excitement   happiness   sadness

exhaustion   bitter taste   sweet taste

As a follow-up to this activity, children can choose an expression and illustrate a picture where they have displayed this expression. Once completed, the paintings can be shared with other children to guess which expression is being demonstrated. If children are writers, they can label the expressions or even create stories about them. Collect these pictures and stories into a book about emotions to place into the Book Corner. For nonwriters, stories can be dictated to the teacher.

Children can make their own expressive puppets if they choose. Paper plates and construction paper can be added to the Art Center for children to use. Once these puppets are finished, children can use them to make up stories which portray the emotions they have shown on their puppets.

    GA1335

Communicating with Our Bodies—Another prominent way individuals communicate is through body language. This section of the learning center requires a small table and an open area for small group role play. Like this previous segment of the learning center dealing with facial expressions, pictures are an excellent way to demonstrate to children the way people communicate with body language. Should there be an individual in the school who knows sign language, it would be appropriate for that person to demonstrate to the children another way people communicate without words.

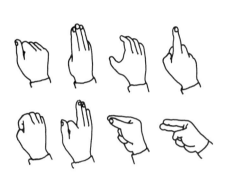

Two or three simple messages using sign language should be available for the small groups of children to learn. The pictures of the hands as well as the messages can be placed on the same piece of butcher paper hanging immediately behind the small table. Since the children are working in groups of two or three, the cooperative efforts should be more productive. While three messages may not be an ideal number for each class, the number should remain small and be kept simple.

Two suggested messages are

"Good morning to you."   "I love you."

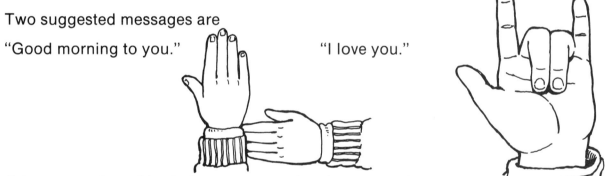

Other examples of body language can be shown on pictures which the caregiver has collected from magazines. Each child should select a picture and guess the message. Others in the group can assist as necessary.

Other Communication Learning Center Ideas—Other communication learning center ideas could involve telephones, tape recorders, walkie talkies, and computers, should the caregiver choose to take a more technological approach to this topic. Proper phone manners and techniques could be stressed. Children should be encouraged to investigate all of the ways that people make and send messages, such as writing letters and notes, telephone calls, walkie talkies, radios, televisions, and computers. Children could also use a cassette recorder to make and send messages.

GA1335

Body Language Task Cards—This activity involves a series of task cards for children to use in role play. Each child is to select a card and use body language to convey the message. After the message is guessed, it is the next member's turn. Sample task card messages are

> To tell a person to come to you.
> To tell others you like them very much.
> To tell a person good-bye.
> To tell a person you are afraid.
> To tell a person you are in a hurry.
> To tell a person to slow down.
> To tell a person to stop.
> To tell a person you need help.

Using Writing and Pictures to Communicate—This activity will require one or two tables with chairs, crayons, pencils, newspapers, magazines, scissors and paper. To introduce the activity, the teacher may wish to share a message with children written in mathematical symbols rather than with letters. When children are unable to tell an individual what the message says, the teacher can tell them that it is because the symbols are not familiar to them. Whether the class members read or not, they can tell the symbols are not letters. An alternative to these mathematical symbols would be a message written in Arabic or any other foreign language.

While the children may not be ready to write in a formal sense, they should consult the manuscript chart in the center if they have a need for print. Children who are writers can write a story that interests them and illustrate it.

A variation of this activity is to have several pictures of people, places, or events available for the children to view. Ask them what message each picture is saying to them. Then ask the small groups of children to create a story using pictures found in old magazines and newspapers. The story can be original or from one of their favorite books. Once the groups have completed their tasks, they can share the results with other children.

GA1335

Sounds That People Make—The teacher should read a message (or have a message recorded) using another language. Voice inflection should be emphasized during the appropriate portions of the message. When the children are unable to understand the message that has been read, the caregiver can ask them what verbal clues tell them something about what was said. Alert the children that when they are working in the section of the learning center dealing with sounds that people make, they are to concentrate on the sounds, not words.

The caregiver will need a cassette recorder for playing sounds that people make as well as a recorder for the small groups of children to make different sounds that people make. Finally, the caregiver will need a series of task cards that call for children to make certain sounds in specific situations and paper and crayons for pictures to be drawn.

When small groups of children begin using this portion of the learning center, they should play the tape with the different sounds that people make. After listening to a particular sound, they should turn the recorder off and guess the type of sound they heard. For instance, the sound may be of laughter, of crying, of pain, of joy, of excitement, or of fear. After making their guesses, the recorder can be turned back on for the correct response. Once they have had many opportunities to listen to the various sounds, they are to record some of the sounds they are familiar with. They can play their tape to other children to see if they can guess what type of sound was being made.

Use situation cards and follow the instructions found on each. Suggest that children make the following sounds:

laughing sounds	crying sounds
sounds when afraid	exciting sounds
telling secrets	happy sounds
angry sounds	surprise sounds
nervous sounds	sleepy sounds

Each child is to take a turn and the other children in the small group are to guess the type of sound being made. Another activity is for the teacher to have a series of pictures with different facial expressions and ask the children to make the sounds they think go with the pictures. This section of the center concentrates on sounds rather than words because of the ways people use voice inflection to communicate their messages.

Sounds That Animals Make—The teacher will need a cassette of animal sounds, at least four animal picture books, paper and crayons. When the small groups of children sit down at this section of the table, they are each to take an animal picture book. Then one of the children is to turn on the recorder and play until an animal makes a sound. The recorder is to be turned off and the children are to look for the picture of the animal that made the sound in their books. When they come to the picture, they can share with the other children to see if they agree or disagree. The tape should then be turned on for the correct answer. Although simple, this provides children with an opportunity to learn more about animals and the sounds they make. By matching sound with corresponding pictures, they are "reading."

Children can select a favorite animal and color a picture of it and where it may be found. Older children may also want to illustrate their favorite animals and write at least one interesting fact about their choices.

Noisemakers' Band—Encourage children to experiment with many ways of using their bodies to make noises. Ask small groups of children to work together to develop a rhythm pattern they can demonstrate on their bodies. If children are successful with this endeavor, they may choose to teach it to their classmates. This activity can be extended by adding household or classroom objects to enhance the "music" (such as spoons, pots and pans, scissors, blocks, paper, etc.).

GA1335

Sound Words Dictionary—Introduce children to onomatopoeia words (words which imitate sounds), and ask them to make a collection of them in a Class Word Bank (collect them on a chart or in a file). Words to include might be *sizzle, zing, bang, pop, crackle, tick, tock, meow, woof, moo, neigh* and many more. Once twenty-five to thirty of them are collected, ask the children to illustrate individual words on pieces of 9" x 12" (22.86 x 30.48 cm) paper. Organize these into a booklet so that children can have a dictionary of sound words in the Book Corner. Children who know alphabetical order could put the words into order.

Later children can experiment with making up poems and choral readings using the sound words. Many of the outcomes of this activity will be nonsensical. Adding motions to the poetry creations will make them more fun. Children can use the activity titled Noisemakers' Band to accompany their rhymes as well. Small groups of children can teach their poems to the larger class if they want. An example is this one:

Sizzle, sizzle, clap!	(pat knees twice, then clap)
Frizzle, frizzle, pop!	(shake hips twice, then clap)
Tingle, jingle, crinkle, wrinkle,	(twist body in all types of contortions in time with the words)
Join us in our hop!	("join us" motion to the audience)
Mumble, mumble, shriek!	(pat knees twice, show expression of fear)
Creaky, creaky, splat!	(shake hips twice, then slap thighs)
Tingle, jingle, crinkle, wrinkle	(repeat motions as above)
Hear the hissing cat!	(place hand to ear as if listening)
Trickle, trickle, boom!	(pat knees twice, make large clapping movement)
Cackle, cackle, pop!	(shake hips twice, then make popping clap)
Tingle, jingle, crinkle, wrinkle,	(repeat motions as above)
Hurry, get the mop!	(run in place)

If children want to write down their sound poems, they can use the Sound Words Dictionary to assist them in their writing. If the poems are bound together in booklet form, recording the poems to accompany the booklet could be a strong motivator to the nonreader to make sense of the sound/print connection in a nonthreatening way.

GA1335

Classroom Printing Press—Bring in an ink pad and printing materials (these kits are available at low cost from a number of educational catalogs and at many toy and variety shops). Let children experiment with writing their names or their peers' names with the print. Some children who are reading will begin experimenting with other messages. Making a mini newspaper for the classroom could become one project that a small group of children would find challenging.

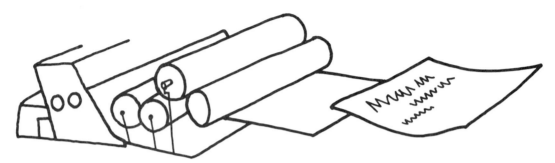

Advertising and Propaganda—Second graders will enjoy investigating propaganda devices which are commonly used by advertisers in television, radio, magazines and on billboards. Some of the more popular types are

Endorsement (a celebrity advertises the product)
Bandwagon (everyone is using the product)
Catchy slogans (sometimes humorous)
Snob appeal (only rich and famous use the product)
Plain folks talk (appeals to common people)

After these devices are explained to the children, ask them to find examples of a variety of types in magazines to prepare a collage representing different types. If children want to, they could also use poster board or tagboard to develop their own advertisements representing real or fictional products.

108

Sounds of the Day—Assist children in realizing that they are virtually surrounded by sound throughout the day and yet may never be aware of them by making a recording of sounds that could be heard in the children's neighborhood, in a city or town, in the classroom, and in a typical home. With the tape placed on a table, the children are to listen to each section of the tape and answer the following questions:

What are some of the sounds you heard?
Do you know where these sounds came from?
Have you heard these sounds before?

Older children can write their answers. Younger children can either record or illustrate their answers. As in the other section, children's books provide an invaluable guide in helping to identify the sounds being heard.

Another activity is for the children to go on a walking tour of different locations around the school (cafeteria, play area, principal's office, nurse's office, bus loading area, etc.), tape what they hear and then begin classifying the types of sounds heard in each location. For instance, the children may hear talking and laughter in the cafeteria, moans and groans in the nurse's office, teachers shouting instructions in the bus area, boisterous children on the playground, etc.

Sounds of the Night—For the purpose of basic comparisons, this section of the learning center should be modeled after the one dealing with sounds of the day. In fact, the caregiver could use the same locations for the night recording sessions as used for the Sounds of the Day activity. Efforts should be made to record sounds found in both urban and rural settings. Again, the children will be asked to listen to a tape recording of the different sounds at different locations and try to identify as many of the sounds as possible. When the tape in the rural setting is played, the children will be surprised at all of the animal and insect sounds they will hear. Attempts should be made to answer the following:

What different sounds did you hear?
Where do you think these sounds came from?
Have you heard these types of sounds before?

When children have been exposed to both activities, ask them to write a comparison story about both types of sounds or make a collage of often-heard sounds of their day.

Books for the Communication and Sounds Center:

Ahlberg, Janet, and Allan Ahlberg. *The Jolly Postman or Other People Letters.* New York: Little, Brown and Co., 1986.

Martin, Bill, Jr., and John Archambault. *Chicka Chicka Boom Boom.* New York: Simon & Schuster, 1989.

Protecting the Environment Center

Earth Day 1990 emphasized the need for mankind to "clean up their act." In order to preserve the integrity of the earth's water, forests and the atmosphere, everyone needs to become more conscious of the damaging effects of litter, garbage, pollutants, overuse of natural resources, acid rain and the erosion of the ozone layer.

Young children will inherit our problems, and a unit of study about protecting the environment is a step in solving the multiple problems which will exist when children become adults. By helping children become more aware, knowledge will go home to parents and, together, families can clean up one small part of the world.

The purposes of the Protecting the Environment Center are as follows:

To help children understand the value of preserving our world's natural resources

To develop an awareness of damaging effects to the world and how people can offset them

To provide opportunities for children to practice what they have learned

To develop an "I-can-solve-it" attitude in children

To help children become advocates for environmental concerns in their homes and in the community

Here's what you need to prepare a Protecting the Environment Center.

Tables and chairs

Bulletin board to display pictures and children's artwork

Trash bags (biodegradable, of course)

Boxes to collect litter (glass, paper products, aluminum products and other trash are the usual categories of collection)

Scrap box to collect scrap paper items for future art projects (this box may be kept in the Art Center on a regular basis)

Picture collections of endangered species of wildlife, examples of pollution, people working to clean up their environment, etc.

GA1335

A typical floor plan for the Protecting the Environment Center might look like the following:

Here are some ideas to try to enhance language learning.

Introducing the Problem—Take a paper sack and pick up several items on the playground area (or in the area around the school grounds) and bring into class. Items should include paper, cans, sticks, leaves, gum wrappers and any other materials deemed appropriate. Place the sack on a table in the center and gather the children around. Ask them what they think you have in the sack. After several guesses, empty the contents on the table and ask them to guess where all of the things were found. Then ask the children if these items have a name. Once the word *litter* is used, the caregiver should find out what the children know about it.

An easy way to determine knowledge in this area is to see if they can place the trash in different categories (for example, sticks and leaves together, cans together, glass objects together, paper objects together).

111

Recycle Center—Children are never too young to begin learning about the importance of our environment and the role they can play in keeping it clean. The teacher should have four cardboard boxes, one for each of the various items that can be recycled and one for those that cannot be recycled: glass, paper products, aluminum products and other trash.

While *biodegradable* is a term that young children will not be able to understand easily for developmental reasons, the caregiver can introduce it and point out that if certain objects are buried, they will disappear over time while others (such as plastics) will not. Those items that do not disappear are considered to be less beneficial for our environment. An interesting science experiment is to bury a number of different items in one corner of the school's playground, checking it in a month's time to observe firsthand what has happened to the materials.

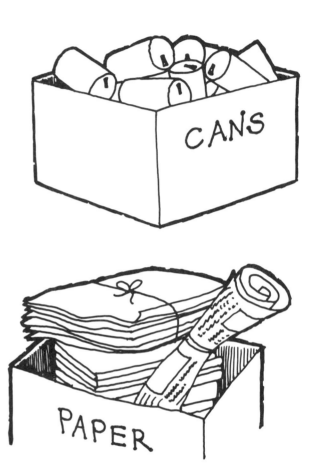

The term *recycle* should also be introduced to children (or reintroduced). The children can begin thinking about separating certain types of cans and paper for the purpose of recycling. To reinforce this concept, product cards can be developed that show pictures of items that may or may not be used for recycling (pictures include cans, sticks, paper objects, plastics, dirt, etc.). Each small group can examine the pictures and group them accordingly.

Call attention to the boxes in the center which are to be used when trash or litter is thrown away. Help children make wise decisions about which items can be recycled and which cannot be.

School Recycling Center—The teacher and children may want to start a school recycling point where papers and aluminum cans are collected from around the school and brought from home. Once a large enough quantity has been collected, the products can be sold to community individuals who deliver goods to large recycling centers. The money can be used to buy much needed items for the school. Another advantage to these efforts is that the parents or guardians will become more environmentally aware and active, and children are developing habits which will last a lifetime.

Where Things Come From—Help children formulate the relationship between finished products and its corresponding natural resource. Examples include different products coming from wood (paper, toothpicks, boxes, etc.), sand (glass), oil, (plastics, etc.), fabric (cotton) and clay (bricks, dishes, pots, etc.). Encourage children to bring other pairs or groups of products from home to add to the collection.

Stow It, Don't Throw It—One activity in the center should focus on litter and the surface pollution of our planet. Litter is so common and many concrete examples can be seen. The teacher can use a dollhouse, blocks to make a pretend neighborhood, or the "plywood community" used in the Neighborhood Center. Regardless of the choice, the area should be completely littered. Small groups of children can take turns cleaning up and messing up during free play. Encourage them to think about how they could stop the problem of litter while they are playing.

Place a series of pictures that represent litter and nonlitter items that are frequently seen around the community in the Protecting the Environment Center. Picture examples can include cans, paper, sticks, wrappers, leaves and any other items considered biodegradable and nonbiodegradable. One child can hold up the cards while the other members of the small group make guesses. Position a self-checking technique on the back of the cards (B = biodegradable and N = nonbiodegradable). This activity is to help the children become more aware of what is often taken for granted. People do not see trash because it is so common.

The Water We Drink—Place several children's microscopes (borrowed from the Science Center), samples of water found in the area of the school, several coffee cans, sand, food coloring and bowls, and any type of white or light-colored flowers on the table in the Protecting the Environment Center.

Show the children several water samples the teacher has collected around the area of the school. The water should be from drinking sources, ditches, ponds, lakes, etc. Demonstrate to the children how they can place a drop of water on the slide with an eyedropper and look at it under the microscope. In most cases children will observe small organisms on the slide. They can use fingerprint art to show what they have observed. Fear is not the purpose of this activity, but awareness by the children that they should be concerned about the water they drink or that animals drink or that fish live in.

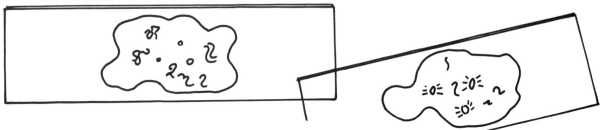

Children can also see what happens to polluted water when it passes through the soil. To demonstrate this, coffee cans (with holes drilled in the bottom of the container) can be used. Each small group of children is to take a coffee can and put sand in it. With one child holding the coffee can over a bowl, another child is to take colored water (either mixed by the children or caregiver) and pour on top of the sand. The children are then to observe how the water looks when it passes through the sand.

Some of the color of the water will be retained while some will remain in the soil. The purpose of this activity is to help children understand that polluted water can stay in the soil and also go to underground water supplies (the concept must be kept as simple as possible). Another experiment at this table demonstrates to the children that polluted water can affect our plants. Small groups of children should take a light-colored or white flower (carnations work best) and place it in a small container of water that also contains food coloring. Ask the children to talk about what they think will happen. In a day or two, the flower will start turning the color of the water, demonstrating to the children that polluted water can affect plants. Since the children are playing junior scientists, have each small group illustrate what happened to the flower (how it looked when it was put in the colored water, how it looked the second day, third, etc.). Their finished projects can be displayed around the room or on the bulletin board in the center. The major point of this experiment is for children to understand that what we put on the ground affects plants and many times water supplies.

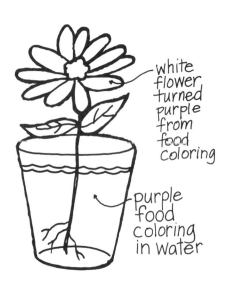

white flower turned purple from food coloring

purple food coloring in water

114

GA1335

The Air We Breathe—Even though we may not see the pollution in the air that can affect us, it is there. To acquaint children with air pollution, the teacher should take several containers and place rags in them that have either been soaked or exposed to different products that are found in the air. Several suggestions for the containers are perfume, paint, smoke, exhaust fumes (accomplished by holding a rag over a car's exhaust while the engine is running for a few minutes; should not be attemped in an enclosed area), hair spray, air freshener, foods, vinegar, etc. Then the containers are to be sealed until the children are ready for this segment of the learning center.

When small groups of children are using this center, they should take the top off of each container, briefly smell the contents and replace the lid. Using a card with pictures of the products being explored, the children should then identify the product or food they think they have smelled. Then they will use the information they have learned about air pollution to predict whether or not this type of air would be safe to breathe.

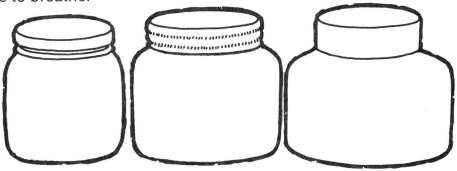

As a follow-up for this section of the center, the children should take tagboard or construction paper to make signs that warn people against using or exposing themselves to air pollutants (sign for no smoking, no aerosol cans, no automobile fumes, etc.). It is important for the caregiver to stress to the children that not all smells are bad or harmful (like the smell of food cooking or flowers or certain types of fragrances) and that just because an individual cannot see the particles in the air, we should not think that the air is automatically safe.

Actions Speak Louder Than Words—Take a walk around the school grounds with the children. Encourage the children to look for any object that could be harmful to the environment. Upon returning to the classroom, the caregiver and children should determine whether or not the school needs an environment plan. Should there be locations where there is trash, the children may want to make a sign that reminds people to take pride in their school and put the trash in a proper container. Also, a letter could be written to the school board or center director to tell about the need for environmental protection.

Home Check—The children who are interested could develop a checklist which would be taken home to evaluate the home environment. The teacher will provide tagboard and help the children label the left column with words and/or pictures for aluminum cans, paper in yard, glass containers, dirty water in ditch, etc. The children evaluate by drawing a happy face or sad face by the appropriate category.

If all children participate in the activity, the results of the Home Check could be compiled on a large chart in the Protecting the Environment Center.

Home Check	
Aluminum cans	✓ 9 cans
Paper in yard	✓
Glass containers	✓ 1 bottle
Dirty water in ditch	None

Look What I Found—Ask children to pick up items they feel could be classified as litter and then discuss why with other students in the room. With the caregiver's guidance, the children will become more concerned with the appearance of their immediate environment and transfer this concern to other locations in the school and on the playground, as well as at home. Point out to the children that people around the world are facing this problem. Once a sizable amount of litter has been collected, use it to make litter collages. Encourage children to write labels or sentences describing their collages.

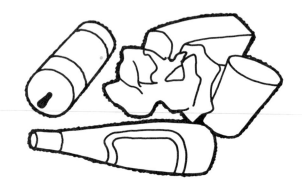

GA1335

A Plan for Action—To apply all of the things children have learned about protecting the environment, there should be an art table set up for a class poster quilt to be made. To accomplish this, the caregiver will need enough poster board squares (12" [30.48 cm] square) for each child in the class, yarn for sewing the squares together, paints or crayons and a hole punch. Small groups of children should take poster board squares and illustrate one solution for each of the types of pollution studied in the center. For instance, the children may illustrate pictures of people throwing their trash into a garbage container rather than on the ground, of separating items to be recycled, of drinking clean water or not pouring something dangerous to the environment on the ground, or of not smoking or of using car pools instead of everyone driving cars and trucks. Use the hole punch to place holes all around the square.

Once the squares are completed, use yarn to stitch the squares together to make an environmental quilt for display in the classroom or school.

Books for the Protecting the Environmental Center:

50 Simple Things Kids Can Do to Save the Earth. New York: Andrews and McMeel, A Universal Press Syndicate Company, 1990.

Peet, Bill. *The Wump World.* Boston: Houghton Mifflin Company, 1970.

Farm and Ranch Center

Talking about cowboys and cowgirls, rodeos and farm animals is a topic of interest to young children. The American heritage was born in agriculture, and the pioneering spirit is prototyped by the image of a rough-and-tough cowhand. Many communities in the West, Southwest and Midwest have regular celebrations of the cowboys' contributions to America. These celebrations lend themselves naturally to a study of farm and ranch activity.

Even for children who live in large cities, learning about their rural neighbors is timely, because their lives depend on the food and commercial products which farmers and ranchers provide. So the study of farm and ranch becomes not only a study of culture, but a study of economics as well.

The purposes of the Farm and Ranch Center are as follows:

To acquaint children with life in rural America and how it contributes to the larger culture

To provide children with as many concrete experiences as possible in order to learn what farmers and ranchers do

To help children understand the special problems farmers and ranchers have because of the jobs they hold

To give children insight about the routines and activities which occur on farms and ranches

To provide opportunities for children to talk and write about knowledge they are acquiring about farms and ranches

Here's what you need to prepare a Farm and Ranch Center.

Table and chairs

Large bale of hay, if possible (place a large piece of plastic under it so that hay will not be strewn around the room in the process of moving it)

Bulletin board to display pictures of farmers, ranchers and animals

Ropes, a wagon, a branding iron, tools used in work routines, such as a hoe, a rake, a pitchfork (use these with caution)

Clothing which would be worn by farmers and ranchers (hats, chaps, work gloves, bandanas, cotton shirts, belts, boots, etc.)

Examples of food which are fed to animals

Saddle, horse blanket and reins (displayed on a sawhorse)

118

A typical floor plan for the Farm and Ranch Center might look like the following:

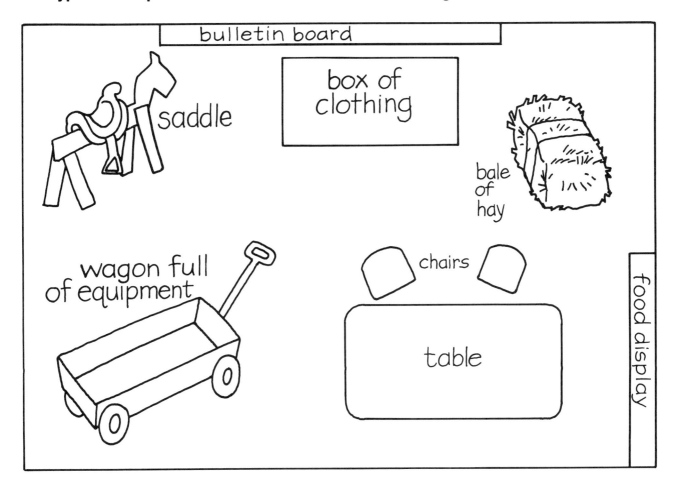

Here are some ideas to try to enhance language learning.

Animals on a Farm—Acquaint the children with the many animals raised on a farm and the products we receive from them by displaying empty product containers and pictures of different types of meat and dairy products on a large table in the Farm and Ranch Center. Beside the product display should be pictures of the animals being studied, or they could be displayed on the bulletin board. Should the teacher choose, a cassette tape of animal sounds could be added.

Ask the children to take the product containers and identify at which meal they are usually eaten. Allow children to express individual preferences for the foods which are displayed. Ask children to match the product materials with the appropriate animals who supply the products.

A PIG

A pig is a farm animal. Pigs are raised for meat. They like to be in mud.

Play a cassette tape of animal sounds and, the children can match the animal to the sound being made. At this point, the children should be prompted to learn more about these animals. Older children can read books about farm animals while the younger children can have the books read to them or listen to them on a cassette recorder. Each small group should be able to identify ways these animals help us. If this topic of study is being studied by an older group of children in the school, they could be invited to the room to read to the younger children as well.

Animal Product Board—Small groups of children should construct a farm animal product board. Either through drawing or painting (or using pictures from magazines), the animal chosen should be represented on a piece of tagboard with the background including the place it might live. At this point, product boxes (when possible), product pictures and pieces of wool fabric or leather can be glued on the board with the painting. The older children can write brief stories about the animal including some of the information they learned from the books, while younger children can dictate or record their own stories. Once completed, each group will be able to share what they have learned about farm animals.

GA1335

Crops on a Farm—The teacher should bring in as many types of grains and seeds as possible. In many cases, this will provide the children with their first opportunity of seeing these products prior to processing. The children should be allowed to feel the texture and smell each. Probably the most easily recognized grain will be corn. On another section of the table, product containers and pictures made from these grains should be available (oatmeal and oats, flour and wheat, cornmeal and corn, etc.).

Small groups of children can guess which grain is responsible for which product. As a checking device, a piece of the grain can be taped out of sight on the product lid. Older children can read the product labels.

Four and five-year-olds could use small samples of the grain to make crayon rubbings. Place large pieces of manila paper over small handfuls of grain on newspaper in the Art Center and rub crayons over the paper. The teacher can write the type of grain which was used on each child's paper.

Remember to use the grain to feed birds in the classroom or on the playground, emphasizing that this food should never be wasted.

Another product board should be developed by the children. Children can write the names of grain samples on tagboard and then glue pictures or labels of other foods that are made from these grains. Any additional information learned about the products can either be written, dictated or illustrated on the product board.

Rodeo Time!—Talk about rodeos as a pastime enjoyed by farm and ranch hands. These events are still popular in some areas of the country, and young children will find pleasure in acting out rodeo time.

Use paper and markers to prepare flyers for the upcoming rodeo, for marking sections of the rodeo arena stands, and for numbering the order of the events which will be presented to the audience.

GA1335

Contour Farming—A simple science experiment to demonstrate the reasons why farmers use contour farming is appropriate for this center. When farmers prepare the land for planting and when the crops are still small, there is nothing to protect the good soil from washing away during a hard rain. Therefore, farmers planting on sloping ground will use contour farming to minimize erosion and crop damage. To demonstrate the concept of erosion and contour farming, all the caregiver needs are two large rectangular pans, dirt and a plant watering device.

On a small table, the teacher will place dirt in each pan and pack it to keep it from moving when the containers are tilted. Using a spoon, vertical rows should be made in one pan, with semicircle rows being made in the other. A ruler can be placed on the lower edge of each pan to demonstrate to the children the depth of the soil prior to the simulated rain.

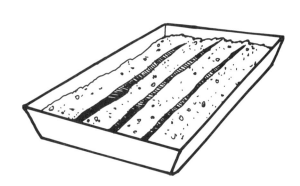

Then the watering can should be filled and poured slowly over each container of soil, making sure that the same quantity of water is used on both. The children can observe which type of row was most effective in preventing erosion. While relatively simple, it demonstrates to the children that even farmers apply science to help their crops grow.

Because of the saturation of the soil, a sieve may have to be used to let the water drain prior to further use. As a result, a reserve supply of dirt may be in order.

Ask children to record the results of the experiment in a content journal, or they may simply draw a picture of what they learned.

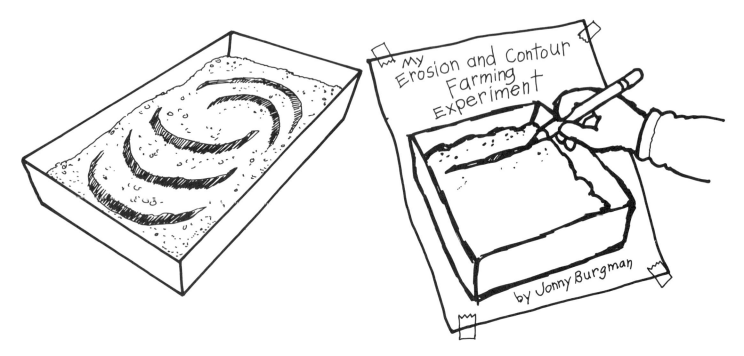

GA1335

Vegetables and Fruits Grown on a Farm—The teacher should provide pictures of fruits and vegetables and actual fruits and vegetables on a table where the children can examine and explore the items being displayed. When appropriate, the children should be allowed to taste samples of the fruits and vegetables being displayed. Because of the perishable nature of these food items, time restrictions will need to be enforced (remember to save decaying food items for a compost heap on the playground).

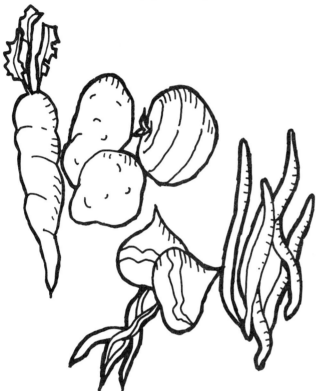

The caregiver should provide paints, shredded paper and tagboard for the children to create their own pictures of vegetables or types of fruits being grown on vines or trees or even underground (like potatoes or turnips or carrots or peanuts). The children can look at the pictures of the vegetables and choose the paint colors necessary for their fruits or vegetables. Children are to dip a handful of the shredded paper into the tempera paint, and let it dry. Colored construction paper can be used for the stems, trees or vines. While the children are waiting for their shredded paper to dry, the rest of the project can be completed. Once the paint dries, the fruits or vegetables can be formed and placed on the painting. The children should also be encouraged to share any information they learned about their products through the process.

Books for the Farm and Ranch Center:

Bellville, Cheryl Walsh. *Round-Up.* Minneapolis: Carolrhoda Books, Inc., 1982.

Elson, Marilyn. *Puppy on the Farm.* New York: A Golden Book, 1984.

Helweg, Hans. *Farm Animals.* New York: Random House, 1978.

Martin, Bill, Jr., and John Archambault. *White Dynamite and Curly Kidd.* New York: Holt, Rinehart and Winston, 1986.

Patent, Dorothy Hinshaw. *Farm Animals.* New York: Holiday House, 1984.

Williams, Garth. *Baby Farm Animals.* New York: A Golden Book, 1983.

GA1335

Insect Center

Zzzzzzzzzzzzzzzzz! Ouch! O-o-o-o-o-oh! That hurt! Insects are such a nuisance, yet they fascinate children immensely. Somehow these small critters are attractive to children, maybe because insects are usually at the child's eye level. They leap, hop, fly, bite, buzz, flutter and capture the attention of our children. Catching a fly in a jar, spying the first lightning bug of summer, watching a pill bug roll into a ball—all these are pursuits of childhood that provide delightful memories.

The Insect Center is one which is perfect for spring study. Hopefully, it will be an area of study which will keep children preoccupied with learning instead of counting the days until school is over.

The purposes of the Insect Center are as follows:

To help children learn the characteristics of insects

To extend children's knowledge of the animal world

To help children learn that insects, though pesky animals, are actually essential to the environmental chain

To provide opportunities for children to learn classification skills

To provide opportunities for children to talk, read and write about insects

To assist children in becoming more aware of safe and dangerous insects

To help children know what to do when they have been stung by an insect

Here's what you need to prepare an Insect Center.

Table and chairs

Magnifying glass and collections of animals

Ant farm (borrow the one from the Science Center)

Books about insects which provide large, colorful pictures for children to look at

Assortment of containers to keep insects in

Bulletin board to display pictures of insects

Journals for each child so that information which is being learned can be recorded

A typical floor plan for the Insect Center might look like the following:

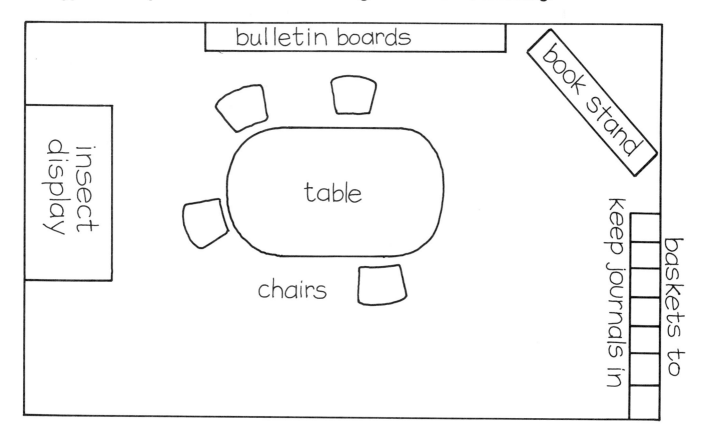

Here are some ideas to try to enhance language learning.

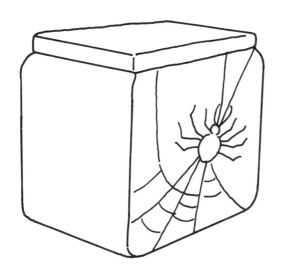

Insect Display Table—One of the quickest ways to involve children in the study of insects is by asking them to bring different types to class. A note should be sent home describing the learning center and how the parents' assistance in the capture of insects could help the children to learn more. Caution should be used in dealing with spiders, wasps and other potentially dangerous species. While live insects would be preferred, they are not essential. For safety reasons, the insects should be placed in a clear plastic container with small holes for air.

GA1335

Once received at school, the containers should be placed on a display table where students will have opportunities to view all of the insects found. Encyclopedias should be available for children to look through to try to identify what they have brought to school. Each small group of children should use the materials to identify as many of the insects as possible prior to actual disclosure. Encourage younger children to look for pictures that look like the insects that have been brought to class. Older children can provide additional facts about the insects.

The next task for the children to undertake is to try to find similarities among the insects. For the purpose of guiding their observations, have them count the legs, look for wings, look for antennae and distinct body segments. Any observations can be written or drawn on a piece of paper. Should there be a wide variety of insects, ask the children to look for insects like other ones and to look for those not like any of the others. While rather simple, this is the beginning of classification skills and conceptionalization processes for the children.

dragonfly

The dragonfly and the firefly both have 4 wings.

firefly

Once all of the children have opportunities to spend time with this section of the center, the teacher should identify the names of the insects from the information found by the children. This would also be a good opportunity to broadly classify insects like others. Rather than formal names, though, simple categories should be established (types of butterflies, types of ants, types of insects with wings, etc.).

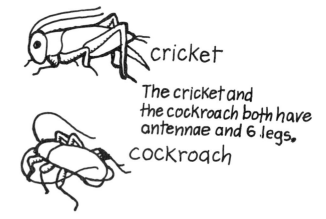

cricket

The cricket and the cockroach both have antennae and 6 legs.

cockroach

Using the information the children learned when identifying the insects, have them illustrate their favorites using finger paint and create short stories about these including any factual information they can remember. Again, for nonreaders, illustrations are sufficient.

Insect Content Journal—When children finish their study each day, ask them to record one or two sentences in their content journals about what they learned that day. Younger children will need to draw the knowledge they are acquiring, of course, but older children should be able to write a precise description of the knowledge they learned that day. Pictures are appropriate as well for older children, if they so choose.

Busy as a Bee—The caregiver should bring to school beekeepers' protective clothing, the smoking device beekeepers use, a box where bees are kept, a blooming wild flower (if possible) and a honeycomb. Small groups of children should be allowed to explore all of these materials and then to tell the teacher what they think the items are. All sorts of pictures and materials on bees should be available for the children to look through. They can see what honeybees actually look like, what all of the equipment is actually used for and other places they may live. In addition, the children should be able to make the connection between the flower and the other items.

The teacher should place magnifying glasses and samples of honeycombs for children to observe closely in the Insect Center. Individually or in small groups, children should see what special things they notice by looking at the honeycomb. Ask them to consider shape, the number of sides found and how the comb feels to the touch. Have a container of honey available for the children to sample. Use a cassette to record what children say when they taste the honey. Play this recording later as a reminder of what the children did when they tasted the honey.

Once the children have had the opportunity to explore the bee table, the teacher can have poster board patterns of bees for the children to trace and cut out. The children then could color or paint the bees and pin them on their shirts to signify that they have been studying about bees. If the interest in this center remains high, a beekeeper could be invited to class to demonstrate use of beekeeping equipment and tell the children how bees help the farmer by pollinating their crops.

Where Insects Live—The teacher should bring to school the following items to place in the Insect Center: an ant farm, a mud dauber's nest, an abandoned wasp nest, a honeycomb, an old piece of wood (to illustrate where termites live), a leaf and any other examples of insect homes that have been abandoned and readily found. The child should be allowed to look at each of these structures with magnifying glasses, to touch them and to learn as much as they can about the structures. Encourage the older children to compare the insect homes with the homes people live in (for instance, both protect against winter, store food, usually for more than one, etc.).

Then the small groups should be encouraged to look at the materials available on insects and to find pictures of as many of their homes as possible. As a matter of record, each group of children should draw several unusual insect homes and the insect itself to share with other children in the class. The older children should research informational materials and add unusual facts about the insects on their illustrations.

As a class project, the teacher can take a piece of butcher paper and place it on an empty space outside the classroom and have the children make a collage of insects and their homes. Each group can contribute its work for other groups of children to see.

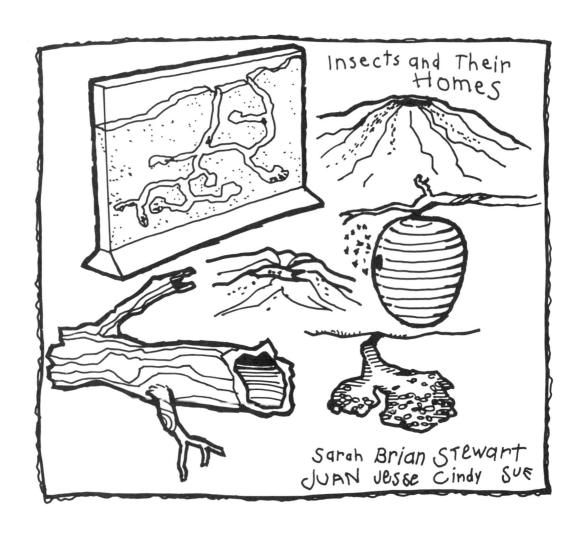

GA1335

Insect Poetry—First and second graders will be challenged to do acrostic poetry using insect names. The words are written downward on the page, and then descriptive terms are added to create an interesting poetry form. Two examples are shown here.

S - cary   G - reat
P - itch-black   N - uisances
I - nsects   A - t picnics
D - angling   T - iny
E - erie   S - tings
R - esting

Feed the Centipede—Prepare a centipede with no legs approximately three feet (.91 m) long to place on the wall or Insect Center bulletin board. Tell children that they can add legs of information to the centipede by reading books and encyclopedias about insects and writing one-sentence facts on centipede "legs" which are placed in the center (or they can make their own). Facts might include things like:

Insects are arthropods.
Spiders are a type of arthropod.
Centipedes are also arthropods.
Arthropods have outside skeletons.
Insect bodies are divided into three parts.
Insects have six legs.
The pairs of legs have joints.
Insects have one pair of antennae.

Those Tiny Critters—Since most insects are small, observation can be very difficult without microscopes and magnifying glasses. Several student microscopes should be available for children to observe several insects on slides and to observe how the small ones look when compared to larger ones. Before the caregiver makes an entire set of new slides, a local junior high or senior high school biology teacher should be contacted to see if existing ones could be borrowed. If not, the collection and creation of insect slides should be relatively simple when using those found in junior science kits.

As the children are observing the insects under the microscopes, ask them to look at the legs, the antennae, the wings, body segments and other characteristics similar to the larger ones. Through written observations or illustrations or both, the children should record what they see. Verification of the types of insects being observed can be made through many of the resource books available. Even if the wording in some of the materials is beyond the comprehension level of the readers, the pictures provide both insight and knowledge.

If the children wish to bring other insects for viewing, they should be encouraged to do so. Also, the teacher can provide a small board (6" x 8" [15.24 x 20.32 cm] plywood) and let the children glue the insects (those that are dead) on the board. After the glue has dried, the children can paint a thin coat of clear nail polish on each insect for a permanent insect collection.

GA1335

Swarm of Insects—Add insect patterns and large pieces of construction paper to the center so that children can trace them, cut them out and decorate in creative ways. If children mix paper colors and add unusual features to their insects, the insects will be quite eye-catching. Show children how to fold them in the middle so they can stand on their own. The pattern can also be used to prepare a large poster showing the three main parts of an insect to be displayed in the center to call attention to the learning children are doing.

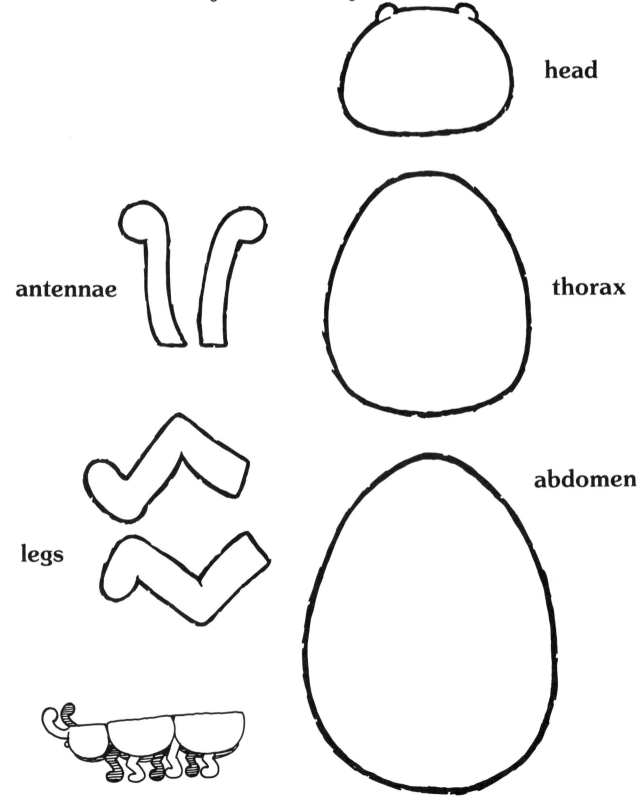

head

antennae

thorax

abdomen

legs

130

Learning Center Extension Idea—If the support materials are available, another valuable section of an insect learning center would be insects of the water. In some communities there could be an expert in this area with materials to share with children.

To help culminate the learning center on insects, the following poem can be read. The purpose of the poem is to point out the ways insects help people.

Insects All Around

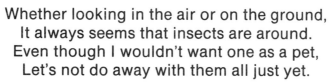

Whether looking in the air or on the ground,
It always seems that insects are around.
Even though I wouldn't want one as a pet,
Let's not do away with them all just yet.

Some insects are helpful to you and me,
Like the honey made by a little ol' bee.
Others are pretty just flying in the air,
Like a butterfly floating without a care.

When the web of a spider is spun just so,
You know there is a fly about to go.
And when there is a dragonfly darting along,
The mosquitoes around are singing their last song.

While a fire ant is very dangerous to touch,
It'll take care of termites, ticks and such.
When bad bugs will not let vegetables grow,
The ladybug is a very good insect to know.

Even though insects are not pretty to see,
Many are helpful to you and me.
It's still not safe to reach down and touch,
But to the helpful bugs—thank you very much!

Books for the Insect Center:

Carle, Eric. *The Very Busy Spider.* New York: Philomel Books, 1984.

Selsam, Millicent E. *Backyard Insects.* New York: Four Winds Press, 1988.

_____ .*Where Do They Go? Insects in Winter.* New York: Four Winds Press, 1982.

Index

GA1335